P9-DVV-187

The Reading Crisis

The Reading Crisis

Why Poor Children Fall Behind

Jeanne S. Chall
Vicki A. Jacobs
Luke E. Baldwin

Harvard University Press
Cambridge, Massachusetts, and London, England 1990

Printed in the United States of America
10 9 8 7 6 5 4 3 2 1

This book is printed on acid-free paper, and its binding materials have been chosen for strength and durability.

Library of Congress Cataloging-in-Publication Data

Chall, Jeanne Sternlicht, 1921–
The reading crisis : why poor children fall behind / Jeanne S. Chall, Vicki A. Jacobs, and Luke E. Baldwin.
p. cm.
Includes bibliographical references.
ISBN 0–674–74884–0
1. Language arts (Elementary)—United States—Evaluation.
2. Reading (Elementary)—United States—Evaluation.
3. Underachievers—United States—Evaluation.
4. Socially handicapped—Education—United States—Evaluation.
5. Literacy—United States—Evaluation.
I. Jacobs, Vicki A. II. Baldwin, Luke E. III. Title.
LB1576.C418 1990
372.6—dc20 89–27202
CIP

Contents

Figures and Tables

Preface

My concern with the literacy development of low-income children dates back many years. As a member of the faculty of the Reading Center at the City College Educational Clinic from 1950 to 1965, I worked with hundreds of children from low-income families who were referred for difficulties with reading. Most of those referred to the clinic were found to be reading below their school grade placement and also below their cognitive abilities. My first research on the reading of low-income children was done in the early 1950s when, together with my colleague Florence Roswell, I was asked by the Associate Superintendent of Schools to look into the low achievement of children in fifth grade classes in a school in a lower-income area in Harlem. The Associate Superintendent wanted to know why the reading achievement of these children seemed to be slipping and how they could be helped.

My colleagues and I gave the children a series of oral and silent reading tests to determine their strengths and weaknesses and also analyzed their results on school-administered tests of reading and aptitude. We found that, as with children we saw at the Reading Center, their aptitude exceeded their reading achievement—as many as one-third were reading a year or more below their cognitive abilities. Some needed help with word recognition and decoding; others needed more help with meaning vocabulary and comprehension. With the classroom teacher, we developed a reading program designed to overcome their weaknesses and to develop further their strengths. The program was successful.

Other studies we conducted in New York City schools resulted in similar findings—that the basic potential among children of low socioeconomic status (low SES) was good, and that they achieved well when the instruction was appropriate to their needs. What we found to be true for low-income children was not essentially different from what was true for mainstream children. For example, in one study of sixth graders in low-income schools, we found that greater structure (that is, the use of readers) was more effective for those reading at grade level or below, whereas a wide array of library books was more appropriate for instruction for those reading above grade level; such findings are also reported for mainstream children.

My next venture into the reading abilities of at-risk children as compared to mainstream children occurred during the mid-1960s, when I synthesized the research evidence on beginning reading instruction. Although the data were limited, they were sufficient for me to conclude in 1967 that a code-emphasis beginning reading program rather than a meaning-emphasis program was more effective for most children, and particularly for low-SES children.

In 1969, in a review of theory and research on the relationship between language and reading, I proposed further that low-income children, if taught well with an emphasis on word recognition and decoding in the early grades, would be ahead in the intermediate grades, when emphasis would need to be placed on vocabulary and comprehension. Because of the way language and reading are acquired, the beginning emphasis should be on word recognition and decoding and only later on language and word meanings for most children and particularly for low-income children.

At about the same time I conducted a study with Shirley Feldmann on classroom and teacher factors related to achievement in first grade classes in low-income schools in New York City (part of the U.S. Office of Education Coordinated First Grade Studies). We found several broad factors related to success in first grade reading: excellence of teaching, a sound-symbol instructional emphasis, a thinking approach to learning, and appropriate level of difficulty (neither too easy nor too hard). Again, these factors have been replicated in studies not only of at-risk children but also of mainstream children.

Later, in *Stages of Reading Development* (Chall, 1983b), I synthesized the relevant research on reading and language and developed further hypotheses on the influence of language and reading skills on the reading achievement of all children and of children at risk.

Vicki Jacobs and Luke Baldwin have also had experience working with low-income children. Vicki Jacobs has taught English at the secondary level to low-income students with reading disabilities and English and reading to low-income students at the college level. As a result of her teaching, she became interested in the relation between the development of reading and of writing ability and especially in how that development in the elementary grades affects students' academic success in the later, secondary grades. Luke Baldwin has taught low-income and inner-city children in elementary and high school. His doctoral research focused on teaching reading to elementary school children from public housing projects. He has taught reading and writing to 11- to 18-year-old juvenile delinquents in an inner-city, alternative school; his current work on adult literacy has included at-risk students from all social levels.

Thus we have all experienced personally what these students find difficult and what they can learn if taught well. This book represents a continuation of our long interest in the literacy development of at-risk and also of mainstream children. The findings of the present study echo findings of my first study in the 1950s—that the reading achievement of low-income children lags behind that of mainstream children even though they have the cognitive abilities to achieve better.

It is common today, as in the past, to look elsewhere than to educational research for an understanding of the literacy problems of low-income children and for ways of solving these problems. Currently, cultural and political theories are offered as reasons for the low achievement of poor children and for the lag between mainstream and at-risk children. Although cultural and political explanations may help us understand the broader picture, in the end they must be translated, in practical terms, into what can be done in schools and in homes. Such translation ought to consider the historical findings of educational research—that good teaching improves achievement and thereby can empower *all* children and especially those at risk. This is essentially what we have tried to do in this book.

Jeanne S. Chall

Acknowledgments

Many people made this book possible. I should like first to thank my colleague Catherine E. Snow, co-principal investigator in the project, funded by the National Institute of Education, on which this book is based. She and her research team, Wendy Barnes, Jean Chandler, Irene Goodman, and Lowry Hemphill, concentrated on the home and classroom influences on literacy and language development in the original study (Chall, Snow, et al., 1982). Their research will appear in a volume entitled *Unfulfilled Expectations: Home and School Influences on Literacy* (Snow et al., forthcoming). The present volume has as its focus literacy and language development and the influence of the school—and, to a lesser extent, the home—on this development. It is meant to be a companion to the forthcoming volume by Snow and her colleagues—drawing from the same data but written from a different perspective.

I am also grateful to many others: to Courtney Cazden, who supervised the collection of data on classroom observations; to Carol Chomsky, who developed the language measures and supervised their analysis; and to Marcus Lieberman, who was responsible for the data analysis.

I wish to thank the many graduate students who worked on various aspects of the study: Luke Baldwin, Steven Stahl, and Judith Zorfass helped select, administer, and analyze the reading tests; Rosalind Davidson administered the language measures and analyzed the results, and Jan Hirshberg helped administer the language tests; Barbara Eckhoff helped collect the writing samples, while Vicki Jacobs collected the writing samples, developed the scoring schemes, and analyzed the writing data; and Gail Kearns did the fluency analysis. Special thanks are extended to Jean Chandler and Lowry Hemphill for their data and analysis on school observations on which Chapter 7 is based, and to Irene Goodman and her collaborators, Wendy Barnes, Jean Chandler, and Lowry Hemphill, for their follow-up data on our children when they were in junior and senior high school (reported in Chapter 3).

We are most appreciative of the cooperation of the school system in which the study was conducted. We are especially grateful to the Director of Primary Education, the principals of the schools, and the staff members who facilitated our access to classrooms and pupil records. Most important, we wish to thank the teachers who invited us to observe in their classrooms and answered our questions. Although we cannot identify them by name, our indebtedness to them is considerable, for this study could not have been conducted without their consent and assistance.

I extend warm thanks for the dedication and excellence of the work of Ann Cura and Faith Harvey in the preparation of the research report and the manuscript for this book.

I should like to conclude with a brief history of the origins of the present volume and its relation to its companion volume, *Unfulfilled Expectations: Home and School Influences on Literacy* (Snow et al., forthcoming). Both volumes evolved from the two-year study of the literacy development of low-income children conducted under a grant to the co-principal investigators, Jeanne Chall and Catherine Snow, from the National Institute of Education. From its inception, the study benefited from the interdisciplinary approaches of the two investigators (Chall, an educational psychologist with long-standing interest and research in reading development and problems, and Snow, a psycholinguist with long-standing interest and research in language development and ethnographic studies) and of the other associated faculty. The varied interests, background experiences, and skills of the research assistants, then graduate students at the Harvard Graduate School of Education, also added to the richness of the study. While the principal investigators fully collaborated on all aspects of the study, each concentrated more on certain aspects than on others. Thus, Chall focused on the assessment and analysis of the children's literacy and language development and on the relation of that development to the school and home, and Snow focused on ethnographic assessments in the classroom and on home characteristics that could explain literacy and language development. To state it simply, the figure for one was the ground for the other.

The final report submitted to the National Institute of Education

(Chall, Snow, et al., 1982) received immediate attention and was cited widely. Parts of the study were presented at conferences and published in academic journals and as book chapters. Requests for information about the study led us to believe that it would be useful to researchers and educational practitioners. To preserve the richness of the data and of the interpretations and points of view of the original study, we decided to write two companion volumes. Inevitably, there is some overlap between the two (for instance, both books take from the original study the purposes and theoretical background, a description of the population as well as the schools and homes, the assessments of the children's literacy and language, many of the statistical analyses, and some of the conclusions and recommendations); but such information is needed by the readers of each volume.

We should like to acknowledge with warm appreciation the use in the present volume of data that became available after the completion of the original report to NIE (Chall, Snow, et al., 1982)—specifically, the reading scores, five years later, of the students in the study, supplied by Irene Goodman and her associates, and the reanalysis of the original classroom data by Jean Chandler and Lowry Hemphill (1983) on a grant from the Association of American Publishers. The present volume, particularly in Chapter 7, uses directly many of Chandler and Hemphill's findings in their comprehensive reanalysis. Chandler and Hemphill's reanalysis provides a clearer picture of classroom effects in relation to literacy development over time, and its findings have greater continuity with earlier research on classrooms than do those of the original study (Chall, Snow, et al., 1982; see also Chandler and Hemphill's extensive review of the literature, not included in this volume; Chall and Feldmann, 1966; and Chall, 1987). While we benefited considerably from Chandler and Hemphill's reanalysis, the interpretations and conclusions with regard to classroom factors in the present volume are ours, and they may, in fact, differ somewhat from those of Chandler and Hemphill.

We should also like to clarify the use of "we" throughout this book. "We" usually refers to the three authors of the present volume; from time to time, "we" also refers to the entire research team who, together, generated the ideas and insights that became the original research report. More particularly, "we" also refers to Snow and her associates in our sections on the home and on home and school cooperation, and to Chandler and Hemphill in Chapter 7, on school factors.

Finally, we should like to acknowledge those too numerous to mention here but who have contributed in invaluable ways to our ideas in casual conversations, at more formal conferences, or through their writings. The search for ways to improve the literacy and language of poor children has existed for centuries and has brought forth many explanations and recommendations. We hope that this volume contributes in a meaningful way to that ongoing quest.

Jeanne S. Chall

1

Literacy and Language among Low-Income Children

The focus of this book is the reading, writing, and language development of elementary school children from low-income families. Such children have been referred to as "culturally deprived," "culturally different," "urban disadvantaged," or as living in inner cities. Occasionally they have been referred to simply as being the children of poor families. They are now increasingly referred to as "children at risk." No matter what the label, their educational problem is the same—they tend to perform below norms in literacy on national, state, and school assessments. Moreover, the lag in their reading achievement becomes greater in the later elementary school grades and in high school (Harris, 1961; Hill and Giammatteo, 1963; Lovell and Woolsey, 1964; Coleman et al., 1966; Cohen, 1969; NAEP, 1972, 1981, 1985; Berry, 1977).

This book presents the findings from a study that was undertaken to learn more about the literacy and language achievement of children from low-income homes. Our inquiry addressed several questions: In what aspects of reading, writing, and language do these children do well? In what aspects do they have difficulty? When do the difficulties start? And—most of all—what can be done to overcome the difficulties effectively and to prevent them?

Interest in the literacy of children from low-income families goes back for many decades. From the beginnings of the scientific movement in education during the 1920s, one finds concern for the achievement of these children, along with theories as to why they do not learn as well as those from more advantaged homes (Currier, 1923; Caswell, 1933; Gardner, 1942; Daniels and Diack, 1956, 1960; Weiner and Feldmann, 1963). Among these researchers was Maria Montessori (1964), who developed special methods to prevent problems in reading, writing, and language for poor children who had not yet attended school or had attended erratically.

Surveys and research on children's reading and vocabulary development consistently found that literacy was correlated with the professional, educational, and economic status of the children's parents (see Currier, 1923; Irwin, 1948; Bell and Schaefer, 1957; Bledsoe, 1959; Coleman et al., 1966), and that children from low-income families did generally less well than those from middle-class families (Nice, 1915; Empey, 1956; Malmquist, 1960; MacDonald, 1963). The research and theories on the literacy of low-income children increased during the 1960s and 1970s—the time in the United States of the New Frontier, the Great Society, school integration, and concern for equality of educational opportunity. Reading was a particular concern because of the considerable evidence that it was highly related to most other kinds of academic learning and therefore could be used as an index of general academic achievement. Further, at every grade level, reading scores are highly predictive of reading achievement in the grades that follow (see, for example, R. L. Thorndike, 1973–74; Bloom, 1976).

During the 1960s, perhaps the greatest impact on theories of educating low-income children came from the Coleman report (1966), a large-scale survey of schools and children which found that family background was the greatest contributing factor in children's verbal achievement. Although several of the specific findings pointed to the powerful impact of schools and teachers on the academic development of the lower achievers and minority children, educators and policymakers generally interpreted the findings to mean that the student's home background, rather than the school, was the primary influence on school achievement. This was also the conclusion reached by Jencks (1972) in his reanalysis of the Coleman data.

Essentially the same was concluded from an international study of reading comprehension carried out in 15 countries (R. L. Thorndike, 1973). When levels of reading achievement were compared, it was found that the more affluent the country, the higher was the overall reading achievement of its students. And within each country, reading achievement was higher for students from affluent families than for those from families of modest means. Further, the students from developing, poorer countries had achievement levels, at age 14, about four years below those of 14-year-olds in developed, more affluent countries. It is significant to note that this same gap is reported by the National Assessment of Educational Progress (NAEP) for its 1986 reading scores (Applebee, Langer, and Mullis, 1988). Within the

United States, in 1986, disadvantaged students at age 17 scored at about the same level as advantaged urban students at age 13 (Applebee et al., 1988).

Thus the findings from the different studies tended to confirm each other. What is even more important, the research confirmed the commonsense and intuitive knowledge of both teachers and lay people. Indeed, larger and more representative samplings and better tests and administration of the tests by NAEP have in the five national assessments from 1971 to 1986 (1971, 1975, 1980, 1984, 1986) confirmed what was already too well known: the children from more advantaged families (suburban advantaged) score significantly higher than the less advantaged at all ages tested (9, 13, and 17), and the gaps become greater with increasing age.

The question, of course, is, why do these differences occur? Why are they so enduring and so universal? Many theories have been put forward. We present here some of the theories proposed during the past three decades that focus mainly on language, cognition, and school influences.

Language Theories

One of the widely known language theories of the 1960s was proposed by Basil Bernstein (1959, 1960, 1971), a British sociolinguist, who identified two language codes. The first he called a "restricted code" (one used in situations where a speaker and listener know each other and the topic well and where communication is mainly face-to-face). The second, a more precise and linguistically complex system, he called an "elaborated code" (one used to communicate across various groups and to permit more exact, more abstract communication). Bernstein contended that, although a restricted code is used in informal settings by members of all social classes, an elaborated code is more characteristic of the middle class. Thus, lower-class children are much less likely than middle-class children to learn and use an elaborated code. Bernstein emphasized, however, that this resulted from lack of instruction rather than lack of ability. This lack of command of an elaborated language code among lower-class children would also put them at a disadvantage in reading.

Dave (1963) made a similar point. He found that parents' attitudes and behavior in the home concerning their child's education have a more powerful influence than their social status. Thus, among homes rated as having a lower socioeconomic status, those that had a higher "press for achievement" (for example, language stimulation, exploration of the larger environment, intellectual interests and activities) had children who achieved better in school than those that had a lower press for achievement.

Other language theories were popular during the 1960s and 1970s. Deutsch (1964) and Karger (1973) studied the difficulties in auditory discrimination among low-income children, especially in those who did not speak standard English, and found that ability to discriminate sounds was predictive of early reading achievement.

Dialect differences were studied widely in the late 1960s and 1970s as reasons for the low literacy achievement of low-income children, particularly among black children. Labov's work (1972) on the differences between Black and Standard English received the greatest attention. While Labov found that Black English incorporates sufficient consistency and linguistic integrity to be considered a separate code variety of English, he maintained that black children have both the linguistic and the cognitive abilities to succeed in school. Other researchers, however, suggested that the child's dialect be used as the language for reading instruction, particularly at the beginning stages. Some even produced "dialect readers" (Baratz and Shuy, 1969). The focus on dialect differences as an explanation for low reading achievement diminished when empirical research found that dialect seemed to have little effect on reading comprehension (Simons, 1979). This finding could have been anticipated, for, as Labov noted, "there is no reason why a person cannot learn to read standard English texts quite well in a nonstandard pronunciation" (1972, p. 34).

During the 1980s, educational anthropologists have proposed other language theories to explain why some children have lagged behind in their literacy development. One of the most widely cited is that of Heath (1983), who reported rich ethnographic data on the language and literacy of culturally different homes. The focus of her study was on "culture as learned behavior and on language habits as part of that shared learning" (p. 11). The aim of her work with teachers was to "make school a place which allowed these children to capitalize on the skills, values, and knowledge they brought there, and to add on the conceptual structures imported by the school" (p. 13). Heath's work placed great emphasis on comparing and contrasting the cultures of local communities, with both teachers and students acting as ethnographers. At the same time, the curriculum included many activities that are associated with high-quality literacy instruction. Play with language and vocabulary development was emphasized;

direct instruction in reading in the content areas was incorporated; reading materials ranged from literature and newspapers to recipes and local history; children did a great deal of formal and informal writing; and teachers focused on helping children learn "unfamiliar" information.

Another anthropological/language theory is that on which the Kamehameha Early Education Project (KEEP) was based (Boggs, 1972; Au, 1980; Au and Jordan, 1981). The researchers in this project hypothesized that the lower literacy achievement of Hawaiian children stemmed from a mismatch between the culture of the home and the culture of the school. For example, the home permits children to speak out and help each other, whereas the culture of the school requires students to work independently from the first grade on. While the KEEP program stressed the need for congruence between the culture of the home and the culture of the school, perhaps the most novel component is the incorporation of co-narration or talk story into small-group reading instruction. In many other respects the program appears to be similar to other reading programs in wide use (Au and Jordan, 1981).

Overall, language-based and culture-based theories have tended to explain the lag in literacy achievement of low-income and minority children in terms of language differences (Bernstein, 1971; Labov, 1972) which stem essentially from cultural differences (Heath, 1983). The solutions offered have tended to call for a better match between the language and culture of the child, the curriculum and organization of the classroom, and expectations of teachers for their students (Rist, 1970).

Cognitive Theories

The great national investment in Head Start and support for *Sesame Street* was based on the theory that stimulating preschool children's cognitive abilities would lead to improved school achievement. A recent analysis of the effects of a variety of preschool programs on achievement by Caldwell (1987) shows significant gains by participants in the first and second grades followed by a third-grade slump. Despite Caldwell's findings, there seems to be a growing feeling that preschool programs that focus on the improvement of cognitive and general abilities not only have a positive influence on later school achievement but also produce a decline in antisocial behavior and in high school dropouts (Berrueta-Clement et al., 1984). There is also evidence that intensive linguistic interaction with adults raises both language and cognitive abilities of low-income preschool children (Blank, Rose, and Berlin, 1978).

School and Classroom Theories

There are two kinds of school and classroom theories—those that concentrate on instructional materials and methods and those that study the effects of school-wide factors. The instructional theories are of various types. One type recommends adjusting the reading methods and materials to the children in order to bring them up to national norms. The methods recommended have varied, depending upon the theoretical assumptions of the researchers. In the 1960s, Bereiter and Engelmann (1966) developed a highly structured, direct-instruction reading and language program that was controversial from its beginnings. The program is still in use in the 1980s and has received many positive reports, but its overall merits are still being debated (Stallings, 1975; Chall, 1983a).

Other researchers carried out intensive observations of classrooms and teacher behaviors to find which instructional factors are related to good reading achievement among children of low socioeconomic status (SES). Chall and Feldmann (1966) observed twelve first grade classrooms of low-SES, inner-city children and found that four teacher/school factors were significantly correlated with reading achievement at the end of grade 1: excellence in teaching, a sound-letter emphasis in reading, appropriate level of difficulty of instruction (not too easy and not too hard), and a thinking approach to learning.

A synthesis of the research on beginning reading methods (Chall, 1967, 1983a, 1987, 1989b) found that systematic and direct teaching of phonics in the early grades was effective in general, and especially for those at risk—low-income children and those with reading or learning disabilities. This is similar to the findings of Coleman (1966) and other researchers, who found that optimal methods, while important for all children, are especially important for those who have greater difficulty in learning.

Broader school factors have also been found to influence positively the reading achievement of low-income students. First studied by Weber (1971), such school-wide factors as a strong principal, high expectations that all children can and will achieve, frequent assessment of children's reading achievement to guide instruction, use of phonics, and a large quantity of reading materials were found to benefit the reading of inner-city children. These factors became the focus of the "effective schools" movement in the late 1970s and 1980s in schools with low-income children (Edmonds, 1979).

The various theories, whether they focused on language, on cognition, or on schooling, tended to concentrate either on preschool or on school-age children. Most of the cognitive and language theories have tended to focus on the preschool years, proposing to improve children's cognitive and language abilities before they enter school. The explanation is that if cognition and language are enhanced before children start school, they will be better able to benefit from the regular school programs in reading and other academic areas. The school-related theories have focused either on administrative procedures to bring about better instruction or on specific methods and materials to fit the expected strengths and weaknesses of the children. Most schooling theories have tended to concentrate on children in kindergarten and the primary grades.

These are only the highlights of the variety of theories proposed to explain the lower literacy achievement of low-income children. Although we have described them as belonging to separate categories, there is in fact much overlap among them. For example, we discussed Bereiter and Engelmann under classroom theories, but their work could also have been classified as a language theory. The Heath and KEEP theories, classified here as language theories, could also be classified as school-based theories. Indeed, no matter what the theoretical explanation for the lower literacy achievement of low-income children, schooling is usually one aspect of both the theory and the solution.

Names and Labels

The names and labels used to refer to children of low-income families have been as numerous as the theories. The names seem to change every few years, and often there is a return to an earlier label when discontent sets in. The names used vary by country and by professional group. Most seek labels that are neutral and primarily descriptive; but they soon take on pejorative connotations, and there is a scramble to find a "better" name.

In the 1950s it was common to call these children "culturally deprived" or simply "deprived." Both labels were rejected in the 1960s and 1970s, and the names shifted to ones that were more sociological, such as "low socioeconomic status" ("low SES"). Later, the term "cultural" was revived and combined with "different" to make "culturally different." Since minority status is common among these children, many have come to use the term "minority children." The National Assessment of Educational Progress used the term "inner-city children" in its early reports (for example, NAEP, 1972), while in its more recent reports the term "urban disadvantaged" is used (see NAEP, 1985; Applebee, Langer, and Mullis, 1988).

Some researchers, particularly in England, have used the term "lower class" as compared to "middle class" (Bernstein, 1959, 1971). In the United States "lower class" is seldom used, although "middle class" is commonly used. More recently the term "at risk" has gained favor, although it can be confusing because the same term is used also for children with reading and learning disabilities (or dyslexia, or specific language and reading disabilities) who come from all social levels.

Design of the Present Study

In 1980 the National Institute of Education (NIE) formed a new study area concerned with the education of low-SES children—in the home as well as in school. We proposed a project to them to study the course of development of literacy and language of low-income, school-age children, as well as the influence of the home and the school on this development (Chall, Snow, et al., 1982).* We prepared to study further the question that most studies of low-income children seemed to overlook: Why does the gap in literacy for low-income children (as compared to national norms) become greater with increasing years in school?

Our study had four main objectives. First, we wished to determine the course of development of literacy and language among elementary-age children from low-income families and to find out whether this development differed substantively from that of the greater population of children. Second, we wished to study whether literacy and language for this population would decelerate with increasing years in school, as reported by Coleman et al. (1966) and by teachers and administrators. Third, we wished to study the effects of the home and

*The study was proposed and conducted by Jeanne S. Chall and Catherine E. Snow as principal investigators, with Chall's major focus on the literacy and language development and Snow's on the home influences. The joint final report was submitted as *Families and Literacy: The Contribution of Out-of-School Experiences to Children's Acquisition of Literacy.*

the school on the development of literacy and language. Finally, we hoped to find effective ways to improve the development of literacy and language among children from low-income families—ways that could be implemented by the school, the home, and the community.

As noted earlier, for several decades researchers have studied why children from low-income homes do not achieve as well as the general population in literacy and language—some focusing more on language factors, others on cognitive factors, and still others on literacy instruction in schools and classrooms. In turn, some focused more on home effects and others on effects of the school. The present study differs from those cited above in a number of important ways, as described in the following sections.

A Developmental Model of Reading

First, we based our study on Chall's model of reading development, which views reading as a complex of abilities and skills that change with development. Thus, reading is viewed as essentially different for the preschooler, first grader, fourth grader, high school student, and adult. The tasks set by the school differ at the various stages of reading, and the abilities and skills needed by readers to meet these tasks also differ. Accordingly, the factors influencing reading achievement are also likely to differ with development.

A scheme for viewing reading in this manner was first presented by Chall in 1979 and elaborated in the book *Stages of Reading Development* (1983b). In these reports, reading is conceptualized not as a process that is the same from the beginning stage through mature, skilled reading but as one that changes as the reader becomes more able and proficient. These changes may be seen in the different texts that students are able to read (see Table 1-1), the prior knowledge they need to bring to what they read, the language and processing skills needed to read the texts typically assigned at different educational levels, and the kind of thinking required for understanding and learning from these different texts (see Table 1-2).

Table 1-1 contains excerpts from typical materials that can be read by readers at successive stages. It should be noted that the selection for each succeeding stage contains more unfamiliar or low-frequency words, longer and more complex sentences, and more difficult ideas. The topics and language become more abstract and more removed from common events and experiences at successive levels. Note particularly the difference in language concepts and syntax of the Stage 1 and 2 selections as opposed to those starting at Stage 3 (around fourth

Table 1-1 Samples of writing from beginning to advanced levels of literacy

Stage 1	"May I go?" said Fay. "May I please go with you?"[a]
Stage 2	Spring was coming to Tait Primary School. On the new highway big trucks went by the school all day.[b]
Stage 3A	She smoothed her hair behind her ear as she lowered her hand. I could see she was eyeing *beauty* and trying to figure out a way to write about being beautiful without sounding even more conceited than she already was.[c]
Stage 3B	Advances in technology enabled scientists to design and build new and better space equipment. By the late 1960's, it became possible to send astronauts to the Moon. On July 20, 1969, astronauts Neil A. Armstrong and Edwin E. Aldrin, Jr., landed on the Moon. They walked on the Moon, leaving the first footprints ever recorded by people on a place outside of Earth.[d]
Stage 4	Perhaps the most surprising aspect of physics is that its experiments and theories can be explained by a small number of relationships, or laws, and that these laws can often be expressed using mathematics. The language of physics is mathematics. For that reason, we begin the study of physics with a review of how measurements are made and how mathematics can be used to describe physical relationships.[e]
Stage 5	One of the objections to the hypothesis that a satisfying after-effect of a mental connection works back upon it to strengthen it is that nobody has shown how this action does or could occur. It is the purpose of this article to show how a mechanism which is as possible psychologically as any of the mechanisms proposed to recount for facilitation, inhibition, fatigue, strengthening by repetition, or other forms of modification could enable such an after-effect to cause such a strengthening.[f]

Source: Adapted from Jeanne S. Chall, *Stages of Reading Development* (New York: McGraw-Hill, 1983), table 2-3, p. 39.

a. From S. Mascarone, *Finding Places* (American Readers Primer) (New York: American Book Company, 1980), p. 19.

b. From T. Clymer and P. H. Fenn, "Speck," in *How It Is Nowadays* (Reading 720, Grade 2-2) (Lexington, Mass.: Ginn and Co., 1973, 1976, 1979), p. 48.

c. From E. Conford, "Fantastic Victory," in T. Clymer, K. R. Green, D. Gates, and C. M. McCullough, *Measure Me, Sky* (Reading 720, Grade 5) (Lexington, Mass.: Ginn and Co., 1976, 1979), p. 66.

d. From J. A. Shymansky, N. Romance, and L. D. Yore, *Journeys in Science* (River Forest, Ill.: Laidlaw Educational Publishers, 1988), p. 217.

e. From J. T. Murphy, P. W. Zitzewitz, and J. M. Hollon, *Physics: Principles and Problems* (Columbus, Ohio: Charles E. Merrill, 1986), p. 5.

f. From E. L. Thorndike, "Connectionism," *Psychological Review* 40 (1933):434–490.

grade): Stages 1 and 2 contain familiar, high-frequency words, whereas in Stages 3, 4, and 5 the ideas and language become more abstract and more subtle and the vocabulary is less familiar.

Table 1-2 presents the changes in reading development in terms of what readers can do at each stage, how these processes are acquired, and the relationship between reading and listening. Column 5 of the table shows the later development of reading as compared to listening. Thus the first graders, who can understand about 6,000 words, can read only about 300 to 500 words at the end of the grade—less than 10 percent of the words they can understand when heard. By the end of Stage 2 (grade 3), reading moves up toward the level of listening; but still only about one-third of the words known from listening can be read. Only sometime toward the end of Stage 3 (grade 8) does reading catch up to listening.

Column 3 presents an overview of the major qualitative characteristics and masteries at each successive stage. A useful way to conceptualize these stages is in terms of the relative emphasis of the two major aspects of reading: the medium, or word recognition (alphabetic writing that corresponds to the sounds of words), and the message, the meaning (the story, the textbook, the recipe, the legal document) that is read. Column 3 shows the major shifts that take place at the successive stages—from learning the medium, that is, recognizing the printed words and learning the alphabetic principle, to acquiring a more extensive, abstract, less familiar vocabulary and syntax. Note that a considerable change takes place at Stage 3, grade 4, when the major task shifts from learning the medium to learning the message.

These changes fall into six stages—from Stage 0 (prereading) to Stage 5 (the most mature, skilled level of reading, in which readers construct and reconstruct knowledge from their own reading). Generally, in Stage 0 (from birth to about age 6) the child learns some simple concepts of reading and writing—reading of signs, giving the names of the letters, writing one's name, and pretending to read books. Stages 1 and 2 (typically acquired in grades 1, 2, and 3) can be characterized as the time of "learning to read." In Stage 1 (grade 1), children learn the alphabetic principle—how to recognize and sound out (decode) words in print—and they read simple texts. In Stage 2 (grades 2 and 3), children acquire fluency and become automatic in reading simple, familiar texts—those that use language and thought processes already within their experience and abilities. Stages 3 to 5 can be characterized roughly as the "reading to learn" stages—when the

Table 1-2 Stages of reading development: The major qualitative characteristics and how they are acquired

1	2	3	4	5
Stage designation	Grade range (age)	Major qualitative characteristics and masteries by end of stage	How acquired	Relationship of reading to listening
Stage 0: Prereading, "pseudo-reading"	Preschool (ages 6 months to 6 years)	Child "pretends" to read, retells story when looking at pages of book previously read to him/her; names letters of alphabet; recognizes some signs; prints own name; plays with books, pencils, and paper.	Being read to by an adult (or older child) who responds to and warmly appreciates the child's interest in books and reading; being provided with books, paper, pencils, blocks, and letters.	Most can understand the children's picture books and stories read to them. They understand thousands of words they hear by age 6 but can read few if any of them.
Stage 1: Initial reading and decoding	Grade 1 and beginning grade 2 (ages 6 and 7)	Child learns relation between letters and sounds and between printed and spoken words; child is able to read simple text containing high-frequency words and phonically regular words; uses skill and insight to "sound out" new one-syllable words.	Direct instruction in letter-sound relations (phonics) and practice in their use. Reading of simple stories using words with phonic elements taught and words of high frequency. Being read to on a level above what child can read independently to develop more advanced language patterns, knowledge of new words, and ideas.	The level of difficulty of language read by the child is much below the language understood when heard. At the end of Stage 1, most children can understand up to 4,000 or more words when heard but can read only about 600.
Stage 2: Confirmation and fluency	Grades 2 and 3 (ages 7 and 8)	Child reads simple, familiar stories and selections with increasing fluency. This is done by consolidating the basic decoding elements, sight vocabulary, and meaning context in the reading of familiar stories and selections.	Direct instruction in advanced decoding skills; wide reading (with instruction and independently) of familiar, interesting materials which help promote fluent reading. Being read to at levels above their own independent reading level to develop language, vocabulary, and concepts.	At the end of Stage 2, about 3,000 words can be read and understood and about 9,000 are known when heard. Listening is still more effective than reading.

Stage 3: Reading for learning the new	Grades 4–8 (ages 9–13)	Reading is used to learn new ideas, to gain new knowledge, to experience new feelings, to learn new attitudes; generally from one viewpoint.	Reading and study of textbooks, reference works, trade books, newspapers, and magazines that contain new ideas and values, unfamiliar vocabulary and syntax; systematic study of words and reacting to the text through discussion, answering questions, writing, etc. Reading of increasingly more complex fiction, biography, nonfiction, and the like.	At beginning of Stage 3, listening comprehension of the same material is still more effective than reading comprehension. By the end of Stage 3, reading and listening are about equal; for those who read very well, reading may be more efficient.
Phase A	Intermediate, grades 4–6			
Phase B	Junior high school, grades 7–9			
Stage 4: Multiple viewpoints	High school, grades 10–12 (ages 15–17)	Reading widely from a broad range of complex materials, both expository and narrative, with a variety of viewpoints.	Wide reading and study of the physical, biological, and social sciences and the humanities; high-quality and popular literature; newspapers and magazines; systematic study of words and word parts.	Reading comprehension is better than listening comprehension of material of difficult content and readability. For poorer readers, listening comprehension may be equal to reading comprehension.
Stage 5: Construction and reconstruction	College and beyond (age 18+)	Reading is used for one's own needs and purposes (professional and personal); reading serves to integrate one's knowledge with that of others, to synthesize it and to create new knowledge. It is rapid and efficient.	Wide reading of ever more difficult materials, reading beyond one's immediate needs; writing of papers, tests, essays, and other forms that call for integration of varied knowledge and points of view.	Reading is more efficient than listening.

Source: Jeanne S. Chall, *Stages of Reading Development* (New York: McGraw-Hill, 1983), table 5-1, pp. 85–87.

texts read in school go beyond what the readers already know, linguistically and cognitively. At Stage 3 (grades 4 to 8), the students use reading as a tool for learning, and texts begin to contain new words and new ideas beyond the scope of the readers' language and knowledge of the world.

Stage 3 is distinguished from Stages 1 and 2 in that the reading tasks incorporate increasingly unfamiliar material. From then on (Stages 4 and 5—high school and college), the texts and other materials typically read become ever more varied and complex in content, language, and cognitive demands. In order to read, understand, and learn from these more demanding texts, the readers' knowledge, language, and vocabulary need to expand, as does their ability to think critically and broadly.

Viewing reading as a developmental process had several implications for our research decisions. First, it led to our decision to concentrate on a major transition—the transition from Stage 2 to Stage 3: from learning to read to reading to learn. Stage 3 reading skills are crucial to later academic success, since at this stage and beyond (beginning at about grade 4) students must read texts that contain more unfamiliar words and ideas. Reading science and social studies textbooks becomes an almost impossible task for students who cannot read on a Stage 3 level. Furthermore, Stage 3 seems to be a major stumbling block for various groups of problem readers: the deaf, many language-disordered populations, and children with learning disabilities as well as children at educational risk because of their low socioeconomic status. Thus, in order to study the transition from Stage 2 to Stage 3, which typically occurs in average fourth-grade readers, we selected subjects in grades 2, 4, and 6. We followed the subjects over two years, extending our data collection to grades 3, 5, and 7. In this way we combined short-term, longitudinal data within a cross-sectional design.

The research literature indicates that larger differences in achievement by SES are found in the middle and higher elementary grades; however, most of the earlier research on SES differences had been done on children in the early grades. We hoped that including children over the age range of grades 2 through 7 would help to explain earlier findings that SES differences in reading achievement increased in the intermediate and higher grades (Coleman et al., 1966; Chall, 1983b).

If the factors influencing reading achievement vary at different stages of development, then the home and school influences on this development might vary as well. Therefore, we sought to identify factors that might be significant for different ages and stages of reading, as well as those influencing the entire group of students.

A developmental model also suggested some hypotheses to explain why the reading ability of low-income children diverges from that of the general population after the primary grades. The "fourth-grade slump" predicted for low-SES children by the developmental model of Chall (1983b) has been noted by experienced teachers and administrators and found often in school reports of reading achievement. We wondered if a reason for the occurrence of this slump at about the fourth grade could be that low-income children may not possess the skills and abilities needed to do Stage 3 reading—that is, reading for information in texts that are increasingly complex linguistically and conceptually. Is it possible that low-income children are more able to meet the demands of reading in the primary grades when the task is to learn to recognize and sound out words, most of which may be familiar to them in speech and listening? Could a fourth-grade slump in reading be related to the third-grade slump in cognition and achievement noted among some low-income children who have attended preschool programs (Caldwell, 1987)?

To examine this developmental view of reading we needed to assess a full range of the children's reading abilities as well as their writing and language achievement. Therefore, we used instruments that separately assessed different components of language, reading, and writing. This allowed us to analyze the components and how they developed and interrelated from grade to grade. Through these analyses we sought to identify components of literacy and language that are more critical for the early or the later stages of reading development.

A Within-Class Comparison of Low-Income Children

A second difference between this study and others is that we studied only low-income children; we did not focus on comparing them with middle-class children. Because sufficient data exist on differences between lower-class and middle-class children's achievement and home practices, we decided not to make comparisons between classes but rather to use within-class comparisons. Thus we chose to limit our sample solely to children from low-income families, whose achievement ranged from slightly below average to slightly above average. By comparing low-income above-average readers with low-income below-average readers, we hoped to identify more easily the home and the school factors that contribute to reading success and to general writing and language development or the lack of it.

This strategy enabled us, furthermore, to collect information on a frequently neglected group of school children—low-income children who achieve well. Studying above-average readers from low-income families, those who achieved above national norms, helped us understand how their families and schools might differ from those of the students who were less successful in reading. Durkin (1982) used this research strategy in studying low-income black children who were highly successful at reading. She found that they had books at home, got help with their homework from a parent or someone else at home, and had parents who expected them to go to college. Moreover, many had been able to read before kindergarten, indicating that an adult had provided books, interest, attention, and teaching. Our sample, however, consisted of a more general low-income population, including both white and nonwhite children, and it did not include children at the very lowest and highest reading levels.

Third, rather than studying a larger number of children less intensively, we decided to study a smaller group with greater intensity. We had only 30 children in our total population—10 in grade 2, 12 in grade 4, and 8 in grade 6, who were then retested a year later in grades 3, 5, and 7. The small number of subjects enabled us to use more tests and observations of reading, writing, and language as well as more instruments and more detailed interviews of parents and teachers. Thus we had a rich source of data that could be used to look at the course of development—both longitudinally and cross-sectionally—and at the effects of the school and home on children's development.

We administered the same tests of reading, writing, and language to all the children in both the first and second years of the study. The reading battery included five components of reading—word recognition, phonics, spelling, oral reading, silent reading comprehension—and one test of word meaning. Items for the word meaning test were presented orally and required students to give oral definitions of increasingly difficult words.

The writing measures assessed various aspects of the quality and maturity of the children's writing in two writing tasks—one narrative and the other expository. The writing measures included holistic ratings and rankings of the maturity and quality of the writing samples as well as measures of a variety of traits such as production, content, form, organization, syntax, spelling, word choice, and handwriting.

The language measures assessed various aspects of vocabulary, syntax, and metalinguistic abilities.

The goal of the study, then, was to determine how both home and school affect the development of reading, writing, and language of low-income children during the second through seventh grades. We were further concerned with whether the gains in achievement for the various literacy and language components were the same at all grades or whether they changed with development. Also of interest was whether the home and school influences differed prior to, or following, the fourth grade, and whether home and school affect the same or different components of literacy and language.

Selecting the Population of Children

To help determine the course of language and literacy development among low-income children, we studied a below-average and an above-average group in each of the grades. We were interested in children representing a wide range of reading achievement but not in those who were at the very extreme ends of the distribution. We hoped to exclude children who were learning-disabled, dyslexic, or language-impaired and whose low literacy and language development might well have a neurological basis (see Chall and Peterson, 1986). We also wished to exclude extremely precocious readers whose abilities or experiences in especially enriching environments might have led to very high literacy and language development. Therefore, we chose children who were somewhat above or somewhat below average in reading but still not at the extremes. We selected children in stanines 2 and 3 for the below-average readers and those in stanines 5 and 6 to represent the above-average. (A stanine is a standard nine-point scale which is based on a normal curve and has a mean of five.) In addition, we attempted to select above- and below-average readers from the same classrooms in order to highlight the variability due to home factors. Our selection was guided, too, by a combination of teachers' judgments and scores on several reading tests.

Thus our selection enabled us to compare the above-average with the below-average readers at the various grades and to compare development for the two groups. The fact that we tested each child twice, at one-year intervals, meant that we could also assess whether the gains for the below-average and above-average readers were comparable.

Influences of the Home and the School

Many social scientists and educational researchers who have studied the achievement of low-income children have tended to focus mainly on either the home or the school. Our research design was based on the assumption that both school and home factors contribute to the development of literacy among low-income children and that recommendations for improvement would be more effective if both areas were considered. Accordingly, we collected data about children's lives at home and observed them in their classrooms to find relationships between factors in the home and those in the school that affect the development of literacy and language.

Studying both the home and the school imposed certain constraints. First, we had to secure the cooperation of a school system and of many principals and teachers within that system in order to be able to collect data within classrooms. The teachers who recommended subjects to us and volunteered to have us visit their classrooms during the first year were generally pleased to do so. They were generous with their time in supplying information about the children. The second-year teachers seemed not to be as enthusiastic as the first-year volunteers; however, they did cooperate by completing questionnaires and interviews and allowing the research team to observe their classrooms.

The teachers recommended subjects for our study, and families showed a range of interest and willingness to participate. In some, all the family members were eager to participate and were generous with their time. In other families, mothers were glad to be interviewed, but fathers refused. In yet others, appointments were frequently broken or postponed. Because we wanted to include a full range of typical families in our sample, we persisted even with those who were moderately unwilling and used statistical corrections for the missing data points—an inevitable result of this policy.

This book will be concerned mainly with school influences on the development of literacy and language. The companion volume, *Unfulfilled Expectations: Home and School Influences on Literacy* (Snow et al., forthcoming), will focus on the home influences. However, we do present here those findings from the home that are relevant to the influences from the school.

Plan of the Book

In Chapter 2 we present information on the children, their schools, and their families as well as on the design of the study. Chapters 3, 4, and 5 present the results from the reading, writing, and language measures, and in Chapter 6 we discuss the interrelations among these results. The influences of the school and the home on literacy and language are presented in Chapters 7 and 8; in Chapter 9 we analyze these influences in terms of development—whether some influences are more effective during the earlier or the middle grades. In Chapter 10 we provide a summary of the study, our conclusions, and recommendations for practice and policy. We conclude with an Epilogue which addresses some of the frequently asked questions about the literacy of children at risk.

2

The Children, Their Schools, and Their Families

Our study was conducted in a small city in the industrial northeast of the United States—a city of about 100,000, representing a mix of working-class and middle-class families. The children in the study lived in three low-income neighborhoods. Of the 30 families we were able to follow over two years, more than half had lived in their current residences more than three years, and the other half more than five years. Two of the three neighborhoods were racially and ethnically mixed, composed of relatively financially secure working-class families as well as poorer ones. One neighborhood was predominantly white. Generally, the families expressed satisfaction with their neighborhoods, which were familiar and safe for parents and for children. Most parents had lived in the general area when they had been children; the children frequently visited with extended family—grandparents, aunts, and uncles—still living in the neighborhoods.

The Schools

The schools attended by these children were part of a system with a better than average reputation. The school system spends more per pupil in the elementary grades than all but five systems in the state, and the teachers' salaries are among the highest in the state. During the first year of the study, some of the children were in classes with the same teachers who had taught their older siblings and even their parents. Although the schools were quite similar in appearance, considerable variation was found in other areas, including classrooms, teachers, and parental involvement. Some schools were more traditional or teacher-directed, while others were more open.

At the time of the study, the school system was composed of a student population that was approximately 50 percent white, 35 percent black, and 15 percent other minority groups. The five schools from which we drew our population varied somewhat in their ethnic and racial compositions. For example, in one school black and other minority children constituted about 40 percent of the population, while in another the white population constituted about 87 percent.

Most of the teachers followed reading procedures that were considered standard both nationally and for the district. The reading lessons tended to be teacher-directed; they were generally taught in ability groups within the class using basal readers, their accompanying workbooks, and teacher's manuals.

The resources available in the classrooms, schools, and the immediate community (for example, the quality of the school library and the frequency of field trips) varied slightly. Some of the teachers were more experienced and skillful than others. Some made use of a wide variety of instructional materials in addition to textbooks, whereas others relied mainly on the textbooks. Some presented activities that went beyond the children's abilities—challenging them to greater achievement—while others seemed to offer less challenge.

The Families

The children's homes also varied considerably. Although most of the children's families were two-parent households, some lived with grandmothers or with single mothers. Some lived on very limited means, while others were more comfortable. Some of the families disciplined their children more than others, and the homes varied also in the extent of their organization and structure. Some could be described as more structured, with parents making their expectations clear to their children; others were more loosely organized, and parents' expectations were rarely made explicit. Some parents thought their children's schools were doing a very good job while others expressed disappointment, saying that the schools were not demanding enough, that the teachers should expect more from the children, and that the children needed to be disciplined more.

Design of the Study

Subject Selection

The first criterion for selecting the children was their low-income status, based on their eligibility for free or reduced-price meals in the school lunch program. A second requirement was that the students be above-average or below-average readers at three initial grade levels—second, fourth, and sixth. It was also essential that the families of the children selected would be willing to participate in all phases of the data collection over a period of two years. We wanted (but were not totally successful in finding) children from exclusively English-speaking families. And we wanted to select both above-average and below-average readers from the same classrooms in order to study the classroom effects on students who varied in achievement. Furthermore, we sought classroom teachers who would agree to be interviewed, to complete questionnaires, and to be observed while teaching.

Teacher Recruitment

Teachers were recruited through the School Department, after a number of letters were sent and meetings held to explain the purpose of the project. The School Department recommended schools that served primarily working-class populations and were ethnically representative of the city.

Teachers in 11 classrooms agreed to participate; their initial involvement included consulting with us about recommending appropriate children, providing ratings for those children on various aspects of reading and math skills, and agreeing to let children be taken from their classrooms for the reading tests used to select the subjects. Further, teachers who volunteered to be involved agreed to let us spend several hours in their classroom to observe the children selected; to fill out a questionnaire about the sample children and about their classroom practices; and to let the sample children leave the classroom for administration of the battery of tests used to assess reading, writing, and language.

The cooperating teachers recommended a total of 91 children. From this group, 88 families were contacted for their permission to have their child's school records consulted and screening tests administered.

Family Recruitment

The vast majority of the 88 families contacted agreed to the initial screening of the children. However, many of the children recommended by the teachers turned out to be ineligible for the final sample because they came from homes where a language other than English was the primary language spoken (19 children fell into this category). Another 16 children were not selected for further participation because they had a history of chronic absence from school, because their grades or test scores placed them outside the specifications we set for the study, or because they exhibited a very mixed achievement record which made it difficult to classify them as either above average or below average in reading.

An additional 14 children were not selected because their families declined to participate in the full study. Ultimately, we chose the children who met most of our criteria for inclusion (one family had two children in the study), although five of the families turned out to be not exclusively English-speaking. A total of 30 subjects stayed with the project over the two-year period.

Criteria for Selection of Above-Average and Below-Average Readers

To make our final selection of children for the study, we relied on information from school records and on the results of tests administered by the research team. School records were used to determine what the children's grades and standardized test scores had been, how many times they had changed schools, whether they had repeated a grade, whether they had received special help, and whether there were any other special factors (for instance, comments from teachers about health problems or home conditions, or high levels of absenteeism suggesting truancy or behavior problems) that needed to be taken into account to understand the child's achievement level.

The research team also administered tests of reading to potential subjects early in the first year of the study, when the children were in grades 2, 4, and 6. The tests included the Gray Oral Reading Test (connected oral reading), the Wide Range Achievement Test (WRAT; word recognition of individual words), and the Roswell-Chall Diagnostic Test of Word Analysis Skills (phonics). The score from the most recently administered silent reading test given by the school was also consulted. We reviewed and discussed the scores on all these tests with the child's teacher. Based on the test scores and the combined judgment of the teachers and researchers, pupils in the sample were classified as falling either into the "below-average" group (stanines 2 and 3) or the "above-average" group (stanines 5 and 6) of readers.

Data Collection

One research team collected data on the children's literacy and language development—reading, writing, and language—at the end of the first and second years of the study. Another research team collected data on the children's families and on their classrooms. The two teams proceeded in a parallel fashion, generally unaware of each other's findings. This arrangement allowed the home interviewers to be unbiased in their observations. The following paragraphs give an overview of the measures used by the home/school research team. The measures used by the literacy/language research team—and results of those measures—are presented in Chapters 3, 4, and 5.

Home and Family Data. The home and family research team interviewed all the members of each family who were willing to participate. In addition, they performed a structured half-hour observation that provided a sample of literacy and a task-focused interaction. Part of the observation was a simulated homework assignment which the mother or father was asked to help the child complete. The children were also asked to complete diaries, using a form provided, of their activities during two four-day periods in the winter and summer.

Separate interviews, designed for different family members, focused on the following content:

1. Basic demographic information.
2. Parental education and literacy practices.
3. Children's educational histories and literacy practices.
4. Views of schools and teachers and interaction with them.
5. Educational aspirations and expectations for oneself and one's children.
6. Degree of financial and emotional stress to which family members were subject.

Teacher Questionnaires. Teachers were asked to complete questionnaires about their teaching practices, their instructional emphasis, their frequency of contact with parents, and their time allocations for reading, writing, language, and other areas of the curriculum. In addition, they answered questions about the focal children's specific strengths and weaknesses. We asked teachers (as we asked parents) about their expectations for the child's school attainment and about the kind of job the child might hold following schooling.

Classroom Observations. Each classroom in which a focal child was placed was observed during one hour of reading instruction, one hour of other teacher-led instruction (typically social studies or mathematics), and one hour of less structured time, such as independent seat work.

In the first year of the study subjects were distributed among 11 classrooms, and many of the focal children were in the same classrooms. Thus one hour of classroom observation gave us information about the instruction received by several children in the study. In the second year, when teachers' participation was not voluntary, the children were in 25 different classrooms, which necessitated many more hours of observation. Therefore, we devised short questionnaires to replace the interviews of the previous year. The teachers during the first year (who had volunteered) were, on the whole, superior teachers who were eager to have observers in their classrooms. Although many of the second-year teachers were also excellent, they constituted more of a random sample and thus varied more than the first-year group of teachers. The teachers in the second year of the study were more typical of the entire range of the system.

The classroom data included observations, interviews, and questionnaires, all designed to study the literacy environment that each subject was experiencing in school. Each child was observed in his or her classroom in April–May of the first year of the study and January–February of the second year.

The researchers recorded their observations as narratives in each of three contexts: reading instruction, whole-group instruction in a content area such as social studies or language arts, and independent work, usually supervised seat work. The observers were trained in taking comparable field notes; they practiced with videotapes and conducted paired trial observations in classrooms similar to those selected for the study. They constructed detailed maps of each classroom, noting displays of student work, number and types of print materials, and provision of literacy materials beyond texts.

The researchers recorded other information about the children, their teachers, and their schools (from conversations and incidental observations) in the form of ethnographic field notes. These, together with the child-focused narratives, formed the basis for case studies of the focal children, classroom ethnographies, and classroom ratings.

In addition, the research team collected information each year from teachers. An extensive questionnaire was distributed to each child's classroom teacher in June. In the first year of the study all 11 teachers completed questionnaires; however, there was considerable variation in the amount of detail they provided. In the second year 19 of the 21 teachers completed the follow-up questionnaire. These informal interviews were used to probe for more detail or to clear up confusing responses. "We also added a section to the second-year questionnaire dealing with writing instruction. The teacher questionnaire covered the following areas:

> Classroom characteristics: grade, class size, age range of students, students' ethnicity and socioeconomic status.
>
> Organization of instruction: team teaching arrangements, subjects taught by specialists, teachers' characterization of activities as child-centered or adult-centered, types of field trips, library visits, frequency and types of problems with homework.
>
> Organization of reading: materials used, grouping arrangements and rationale for their use, skills emphasis.
>
> Focal child's reading experience: level of reading competency relative to classmates, factors contributing to this level, reading group assignment, length and scheduling of reading period, texts used, skills focus, and provision of outside help.
>
> Home-school contacts: judgment about whether the family helped with homework; mode, number, and content of teacher-initiated contacts with family; obstacles experienced in establishing communication and effects of these contacts; content of contacts initiated by the family and characterization of family's overall contribution.
>
> Focal child's competencies: language problems or learning disabilities, participation during whole-group instruction, approach to independent work, preferred free-time activities, likely level of final schooling." (Chandler and Hemphill, 1983, pp. 7–8)

Thus, the design of the study consisted of extensive observations of children in their classrooms, reports by teachers in questionnaires and interviews, and detailed observations and information obtained from the child's family. It also included extensive testing once each year of various components of reading, writing, and language. A study of such depth, conducted over a two-year period, could be completed only by limiting the number of children studied—30 altogether. Although we are aware of the sample's limitations, the design of our study allowed us to examine language and literacy development as well as school and home factors in much greater detail than most other studies of low-income children. Through careful longitudinal and cross-sectional analyses, we believe we have begun to determine not just whether a lag exists, but the nature of the lag and *why* it exists.

3

Reading Development

How well did our population of low-income children read? Did they do better in the earlier than in the later elementary grades? Do the children's scores reflect a fourth-grade slump? If so, do all the components of reading slip at the same time? And is the course of development similar for both above-average and below-average readers? In this chapter we attempt to answer these questions through an analysis of the children's reading performance.

The Reading Tests

Reading was assessed by a battery of tests, administered individually, in May of the first year of the study (when the children were in grades 2, 4, and 6) and in May of the second year (when they were in grades 3, 5, and 7). The test battery used was the Roswell-Chall Diagnostic Assessment of Reading and Teaching Strategies (in press), which covers a wide range of reading achievement and consists of tests in the following six areas:

word recognition: reading aloud words of increasing difficulty.

phonics: a test of basic knowledge of phonics, from giving sounds for consonant letters to pronouncing polysyllabic words.

spelling: accuracy of written responses to dictation of increasingly difficult words.

oral reading: a test of accuracy and fluency in the oral reading of passages of increasing difficulty (comprehension questions are not included).

silent reading comprehension: silent reading of passages of increasing difficulty followed by answering multiple-choice comprehension questions.

word meaning: giving oral definitions of increasingly difficult words presented orally by the examiner.

It should be noted that five of the six tests (word recognition, phonics, spelling, oral reading, and silent reading comprehension) require the reading or writing of print. The word meaning test requires no reading since it is administered orally. And the spelling test, although not technically a reading test, requires the use of writing and is thus print-related. We can further divide the five tests that rely on reading or writing into two groups: those that rely mainly on word recognition and decoding and those that rely mainly on reading comprehension and meaning. Four tests (word recognition, phonics, spelling, and oral reading) can be viewed as requiring considerable amounts of word recognition and decoding more than comprehension and meaning. Oral reading, however, although it requires considerable word recognition and decoding, is also facilitated by comprehension. A fifth test, silent reading comprehension, contains the strongest meaning component but is also facilitated by word recognition and decoding. Only the sixth test, the word meaning test, requires no knowledge of print, of word recognition, or of decoding; it requires only a knowledge of word meanings and an ability to express those meanings orally.

Thus, overall, these tests made possible an analysis of how reading developed for children in grades 2 through 7 as measured by various reading components. We were also able to analyze whether children were stronger in the recognition or the meaning aspects of reading.

Reading Results

How Well Did the Children Achieve?

We compared the reading scores of the children in grades 2, 4, and 6 with the expected norms for each of these grades, and found that the children in grades 2 and 4 generally achieved at their expected grade levels.* However, at grade 6, they achieved almost a half-year below grade norms (Table 3-1). The trends were similar on the retests a year

*The four subtests used for this analysis were the print-based tests of word recognition, oral reading, silent reading comprehension, and spelling. The phonics subtest was not used because the scores were not available in grade equivalents.

Table 3-1 Mean reading scores and discrepancies from norms, total population, grades 2, 4, and 6

Grade	Expected (in May)[a]	Mean reading scores (in May)[b]	Discrepancies of achievement from expected scores
2	2.8	3.0	+0.2
4	4.8	4.9	+0.1
6	6.8	6.4	−0.4

a. The expected scores are grade level equivalents. That is, a score of 2.8 means that it is the average score for children in the eighth month of the second grade. It also means that, in general, a child who receives such a score can do the work of most children at that level.

b. Mean scores are for word recognition, oral reading, silent reading comprehension and spelling combined (print-based tests). Word meaning was not included because it was not print-based. The phonics subtest was not included because the scores did not convert to grade equivalents. The highest possible score on these tests varies from grade levels 9 through 12.

Table 3-2 Mean reading scores and discrepancies from norms, compared to expectations, total population, grades 3, 5, and 7

Grade	Expected (in May)[a]	Mean reading scores (in May)[b]	Discrepancies of achievement from expected scores
3	3.8	4.5	+0.7
5	5.8	6.5	+0.7
7	7.8	7.5	−0.3

a. The expected scores are grade level equivalents. That is, a score of 3.8 means that it is the average score for children in the eighth month of the third grade. It also means that, in general, a child who receives such a score can do the work of most children at that level.

b. Mean scores are for word recognition, oral reading, silent reading comprehension and spelling combined (print-based tests). Word meaning was not included because it was not print-based. The phonics subtest was not included because the scores did not convert to grade equivalents.

later (Table 3-2): in grades 3 and 5 the scores were higher than expected, but at grade 7 the scores were lower than expected. Thus, on the retest, the trend was similar to that for the first year—deceleration with increasing grades.

We also wanted to investigate whether the pattern of gains and decelerations would be the same or different for the four separate

Table 3-3 Mean test scores and differences from norms on reading battery, total population tested at end of grades 2, 4, and 6

Grade	Word recognition	Oral reading	Silent reading	Spelling	Word meaning
Grade 2	2.7	3.5	2.9	2.9	3.1
Difference from 2.8[a]	(−0.1)	(+0.7)	(+0.1)	(+0.1)	(+0.3)
Grade 4	4.5	4.9	5.5	4.6	4.3
Difference from 4.8[a]	(−0.3)	(+0.1)	(+0.7)	(−0.2)	(−0.5)
Grade 6	6.1	6.7	6.6	6.1	4.4
Difference from 6.8[a]	(−0.7)	(−0.1)	(−0.2)	(−0.7)	(−2.4)

a. Expected grade equivalents, or norms, for May of the school year.

print-related reading tests. And what trend would we find for the word meaning test, which did not require reading? Overall, the scores on all five tests were closer to grade level expectations in the earlier grades than they were in the later grades (Table 3-3). At grade 2, the children scored on grade level or higher on all five tests. At grade 4, however, the scores began to slip below expected levels on the tests of word meaning, word recognition, and spelling. On oral reading and silent reading comprehension, the fourth graders still scored on grade level or above. Yet by grade 6, scores on all subtests were below grade level. The greatest slump was in word meaning; students scored almost two and one-half years below the norm. The next bigger slump was in word recognition and spelling, with students scoring about one-half year below expectations. Deceleration was lowest in oral and silent reading, where the students scored only slightly below norms. Thus, on the reading (print-related) tests, scores decelerated first on the tests that did not use context (word recognition and spelling). The tests that did use context (oral and silent reading comprehension) decelerated last.

These trends were still evident in the retests a year later (Table 3-4). At grade 3, the children were on grade level or above on all the tests except spelling. At grade 5, two of the five test scores were below grade level—word meaning and spelling. By grade 7, the students were below grade level on all of the tests except oral reading. As in the previous year, the oldest students were the furthest behind in word meaning (by almost three years) and in spelling (about one year below). Only their oral reading was still somewhat above grade level.

Table 3-4 Mean test scores and differences from norms on reading battery, total population retested in grades 3, 5, and 7

Grade	Word recognition	Oral reading	Silent reading	Spelling	Word meaning
Grade 3	4.3	5.2	4.8	3.7	3.9
Difference from 3.8[a]	(+0.5)	(+1.4)	(+1.0)	(−0.1)	(+0.1)
Grade 5	6.9	6.8	7.0	5.5	4.8
Difference from 5.8[a]	(+1.1)	(+1.0)	(+1.2)	(−0.3)	(−1.0)
Grade 7	7.3	8.1	7.1	6.7	5.0
Difference from 7.8[a]	(−0.5)	(+0.3)	(−0.7)	(−1.1)	(−2.8)

a. Expected grade equivalents, or norms, for May of the school year.

Table 3-5 Mean reading scores and discrepancies from norms for above-average and below-average readers, grades 2, 4, and 6

		Above-average readers		Below-average readers	
Grade	Expected (in May)	Mean reading scores (in May)[a]	Word meaning scores	Mean reading scores (in May)[a]	Word meaning scores
Grade 2	2.8	2.9	3.2	3.0	3.0
		(+0.1)[b]	(+0.4)	(+0.2)	(+0.2)
Grade 4	4.8	5.6	4.2	3.9	4.4
		(+0.8)	(−0.6)	(−0.9)	(−0.4)
Grade 6	6.8	7.3	4.5	5.5	4.3
		(+0.5)	(−2.3)	(−1.3)	(−2.5)

a. Average of word recognition, oral reading, silent reading, and spelling.
b. Discrepancy from expected score (norm).

Above-Average and Below-Average Readers

Were the patterns of development the same or different for the above-average and below-average readers? Table 3-5 presents the scores for these two groups of readers at grades 2, 4, and 6 on the four print-related tests (word recognition, oral reading, silent reading comprehension, and spelling) and on the print-free word meaning test. The striking feature of this table is that, although the above-average and below-average readers received about the same scores in grade 2, differences appeared between the two groups at grade 4, and the differences were still greater in grade 6. In grades 4 and 6, the above-average readers scored well above expected grade levels on the print-based reading tests, showing little evidence of deceleration. However, the below-average readers' scores began to decelerate at grade 4, falling nearly a year below grade norms. By sixth grade, their scores were more than a year below norms.

The performance of the two groups of readers on the word meaning test (which did not require reading) was similar at each of the grades. Each group scored slightly above grade level at grade 2; at fourth grade both scored about a half-year below grade level; in sixth grade each group scored more than two years below grade norms. Thus, on word meaning, each group fared equally well at grade 2 and equally poorly at grades 4 and 6.

The comparisons of above-average with below-average readers are important for several reasons. First, they show that deceleration on the print-related subtests, for children from low-SES families, appears to be a phenomenon that is more characteristic of the lower than the higher achievers. Second, they show that deceleration on the word meaning subtest, which does not require reading, is characteristic of both the above-average and below-average readers. Both groups performed poorly on word meaning after grade 3. Third, these comparisons helped us to understand the course of development of the various reading components by grade and by overall reading achievement.

In grades 2 and 3, the reading tests indicated that the children, as a whole, had the vocabulary and the reading skills necessary for the reading expected of them. But in grade 4, two things seemed to happen. First, vocabulary began to slip for all students, for the good as well as the poor readers. Why did both groups begin to decelerate in grade 4 on word meanings? A likely hypothesis is that, at this level, the words tested are less frequent in the English language—they are more abstract, technical, and literary. It is with these abstract words, which also occur less frequently in the language, that both the good and the poor readers had difficulty. However, the above-average and below-average readers differed in their ability to read print, with the above-average readers doing consistently better than the below-average ones. At grade 6, the above-average readers tested about a half grade above norms, while the below-average readers were more than a year below grade level.

Similar trends were found on the retests in grades 3, 5, and 7 (Table

Table 3-6 Mean reading scores and discrepancies from norms for above-average and below-average readers, grades 3, 5, and 7

Grade	Expected (in May)	Above-average readers: Mean reading scores (in May)[a]	Above-average readers: Word meaning scores	Below-average readers: Mean reading scores (in May)[a]	Below-average readers: Word meaning scores
Grade 3	3.8	4.5 (+0.7)[b]	4.1 (+0.3)	4.5 (+0.7)	3.9 (+0.1)
Grade 5	5.8	7.5 (+1.7)	4.8 (−1.0)	5.3 (−0.5)	4.8 (−1.0)
Grade 7	7.8	8.5 (+0.7)	5.1 (−2.7)	6.4 (−1.4)	5.0 (−2.8)

a. Average of word recognition, oral reading, silent reading, and spelling.
b. Discrepancy from expected score (norm).

3-6). Here, too, the above-average readers scored well on the print-related reading tests, but the below-average readers decelerated considerably after grade 3. By seventh grade the below-average readers were nearly a year and one-half below norms, while the above-average readers were more than a half-year above norms. On word meanings, the trends for the above-average and below-average readers in grades 3, 5, and 7 were similar. Both groups of readers were on grade level in grade 3, and both decelerated at increasing rates in grades 5 and 7.

To sum up our findings thus far: We found a general decelerative trend in reading that started around fourth grade. The start of the slump and its intensity varied by the children's reading ability and by the reading components tested. The below-average readers started to decelerate earlier, around fourth grade, and they experienced a more intensive slump through the sixth and seventh grades. The above-average readers started to decelerate later, and their slump was less intense. Word meanings decelerated earliest (after grade 3) and most intensely among both the good and the poor readers. The next to decelerate were word recognition and spelling. The oral and silent reading comprehension test scores held up the longest. Thus, overall, we did find a fourth-grade slump—particularly among the below-average readers and on tests that do not rely on the use of context.

Our research design made it possible to view trends across grades when the students were in grades 2, 4, and 6 during the first year of the study and when the same students were in grades 3, 5, and 7 in the second year. We were also able to view gains for the same students over a one-year period on pretests and posttests. As the tables indicate, the cross-sectional and the longitudinal analyses found similar trends—faster development on various reading measures in the earlier grades and slower development beginning at about grade 4 or 5. The same trends were found when the above-average and below-average students were compared grade by grade.

One might ask, however, to what extent the decelerating trends we found were influenced by the nature of our sample. Could these trends be attributed to sample selection rather than to a real decline with age? Were the older cohorts simply comprised of weaker readers?

The exact numbers of subjects in each grade cohort differed somewhat. The grade 4–5 cohort was larger (N = 12) than the grade 2–3 cohort (N = 10) or the grade 6–7 cohort (N = 8). Further, the grade 4–5 cohort had slightly more above-average readers (58 percent) than the grade 2–3 cohort (40 percent) or the grade 6–7 cohort (50 percent). To ensure that these sampling differences were not influential in the developmental trends that were found, we performed a covariance analysis using reading scores from the Metropolitan Achievement Test for the total sample of students when they were in the third grade. The Metropolitan scores were covaried with one of our writing measures (production) and with the various reading measures.

The covariance results indicated that none of the cohorts differed significantly from the others in relation to national norms on their third grade reading skills as measured by the Metropolitan Achievement Test (see Chall, Snow, et al., 1982, p. 6-2b, Table 6-0). Thus, the decelerating trends could not be attributed to the nature of the sampling itself.

Case Studies

Four children were selected to highlight the differences in progress of above-average and below-average readers from grades 4 to 5 and 6 to 7. We did not select children in grades 2 and 3 because differences between above-average and below-average second and third graders were minimal (see Table 3-6), with both groups scoring at or slightly above expected levels. Table 3-7 gives the individual scores of the four children.

Table 3-7 Cases: Above-average and below-average readers at the end of grades 5 and 7

Student	Mean reading[a]	Word recognition	Oral reading	Silent reading	Spelling	Word meaning
Joshua (below-average)						
Grade 4[b]	4.2	4	4	6	3	4
Grade 5	4.5	4	5	6	3	4
Gain	+0.3	0	+1	0	0	0
Alex (above-average)						
Grade 4	5.0	4	6	5	6	4
Grade 5	8.2	8	9–10	8	7	5–6
Gain	+3.2	+4	+3–4	+3	+1	+1–2
Bill (below-average)						
Grade 6	4.7	5	6	6	2	4
Grade 7	4.7	5	6	6	2	5–6
Gain	0.0	0	0	0	0	+1–2
Janet (above-average)						
Grade 6	7.5	7	9–10	6	7	4
Grade 7	9.5	9–10	11–12	8	8	5–6
Gain	+2.0	+2–3	+2	+2	+1	+1–2

a. The mean reading score is an average of word recognition, oral reading, silent reading, and spelling.

b. The expected grade equivalents are 4.8 for the fourth grade, 5.8 for the fifth, 6.8 for the sixth, and 7.8 for the seventh.

Grades 4 to 5: Joshua and Alex. Joshua represents a typical below-average reader at grades 4 to 5, and Alex represents a fairly typical above-average reader (see Table 3-5).

At the end of grade 4, when the average, expected achievement is approximately 4.8, Joshua showed particular strength on the silent reading comprehension test (more than a year above expected level). However, he scored below expected levels on all other aspects of reading and spelling, lagging nearly one year behind in word recognition, oral reading, and word meaning and almost two years behind in spelling (see Table 3-7).

At the end of grade 5, Joshua again scored below expected grade level on all of the reading measures except for silent reading comprehension, on which he scored at about the expected grade level—but not above what he had scored at the end of grade 4. He scored nearly a year below expected grade levels on oral reading, two years below on word recognition and word meaning, and three years below on spelling. His weaknesses in word recognition and word meaning seem to have limited his gains on oral reading (one year of gain) and silent reading comprehension (no gain).

In contrast, Alex made considerable progress over the course of the year (see Table 3-7). At the end of grade 4, Alex scored at or above the expected grade level on most aspects of reading. He scored at expected grade level on silent reading and about one year above grade level on oral reading and spelling. His scores on word recognition and word meaning were nearly one year below expected levels.

At the end of grade 5, Alex had made gains in all areas tested. He scored above expected grade levels on all reading tests except for word meaning, on which he scored at about grade level. Thus, Alex's developing strength in the more precise aspects of reading (for example, word recognition and spelling) probably supported his progress in oral and silent reading. However, we note that Alex's word meaning score, though at expected grade level, lagged behind his scores on other tests. Later in this chapter we will discuss whether or not such a lag affects children's ability to read increasingly more complex, technical texts in the upper grades.

Grades 6 to 7: Bill and Janet. Bill represents a typical below-average reader at grades 6 to 7, and Janet represents a fairly typical above-average reader.

At the end of grade 6, Bill scored below expected levels in all aspects of reading (see Table 3-7). He scored almost a year below grade level in oral reading and in silent reading comprehension. He was nearly two years behind in word recognition, three years behind in word meaning, and nearly five years behind in spelling. Like many below-average readers in our sample, his relative strength was in contextualized tasks (oral and silent reading), but he was very weak in areas that required precision with isolated words (such as spelling and word recognition). By grade 6 he lagged severely in word meaning; he could only define words of about fourth grade difficulty (such as "nervous" and "sprout") and could not define words typical of sixth grade level, such as "occupation" and "exaggeration" (see Dale and O'Rourke, 1981).

By the end of grade 7, Bill had made few if any gains on the reading measures and thus lagged even further below expected levels on all aspects of reading. He scored nearly two years below expected levels on oral and silent reading (the contextualized tasks), nearly three years below on word recognition, and nearly six years below on spelling (the decontextualized aspects of reading). Although he made modest gains on word meaning (one to two years), his score remained about a year below the expected level.

On the other hand, at the end of grade 6 Janet scored at or above expected grade levels on almost all aspects of reading. She scored at about grade level in word recognition and spelling and more than two years above the expected level on oral reading. Her weakness was in word meanings, on which she scored nearly three years below the expected grade level.

At the end of grade 7 Janet made gains in all areas of reading we tested, although some gains were stronger than others. She scored three to four years above the expected level in oral reading and one to two years above the expected level in word recognition. She scored at about expected levels on silent reading and spelling. Despite these gains, her word meaning score remained two years below the expected level.

Janet's relatively strong scores on word recognition may indicate that she was very adept at processing print and could "read," that is, identify, words that she could not define. Janet could give the meanings of words typical of grade 5–6 reading, such as "exaggeration" and "occupation," but she was unable to define words typical of grade 7–8 reading, such as "solemn," "technical," and "negligence" (see Dale and O'Rourke, 1981). One might predict that in grade 8 Janet would encounter great difficulty with the more abstract vocabulary typical of textbooks at that level.

Summary

Although some below-average readers made slightly greater gains than either Joshua or Bill, their cases illustrate how below-average readers experienced an earlier slump in reading development than did above-average readers and how the gaps in reading achievement widened between the two groups of readers. Both above-average and below-average readers were relatively stronger on contextualized tasks (that is, silent and oral reading) and relatively weaker on the more precise or decontextualized aspects of reading (word recognition and spelling). Neither group of readers ever scored above expected grade levels on word meaning; in fact, in most cases they scored one to two years below.

Beginning at about grade 4, students are expected to read textbooks in various subject areas whose readability levels are often higher than

> You have many ways of learning about the world around you. The sense organs provide information about activities within your body and outside your body. All the sense organs depend on sensory nerves and the messages they send to specific areas within the brain. You have five senses—touch, taste, smell, sight, and hearing.
>
> **Smell** Another sense that is closely connected with the sense of taste is the sense of smell. Where, do you think, are the organs of the sense of smell found?
>
> Both taste and smell depend on chemical stimulation. The taste buds in your tongue and the smell receptors inside the top part of your nose are sensitive to certain chemicals.

Figure 3–1 Sixth grade science text. From James A. Shymansky, Nancy Romance, and Larry D. Yore, *Journeys in Science*, p. 317. Copyright 1988 by Laidlaw Brothers. Dale-Chall readability of full text = 7–8th grade; of passage = 7th grade.

the grade levels for which the texts are intended. For example, a sixth grade science text might have a readability level of grades 7–8; and an eighth grade text might be written at a high school level. Therefore, all four of the children profiled above, and particularly the below-average readers, were at risk of not being able to read the subject-matter texts typical of their respective grades.

Examples of Texts

Figures 3-1 and 3-2 present brief excerpts from widely used textbooks in science and social studies written for the sixth grade, texts that Bill and Janet would be expected to read. Although the textbooks are designated for sixth grade, both have readability levels closer to seventh to eighth grade.

Janet, our above-average reader, with a combined reading score of 7.5, would probably be able to read these texts. However, since her knowledge of word meanings was only at the fourth-grade level, she would need considerable instruction on the meanings of the less common words in both textbooks in order to comprehend them fully. Bill's ability to read these texts would be severely limited. His mean reading score at the end of grade 6 of only 4.7, and his fourth-grade level on word meanings, would make learning from these texts extremely difficult. Lacking skill in word recognition, Bill would probably misread many of the words and would in general have great difficulty in learning from these texts without considerable help.

> Iron changed the lives of the Nok people as it did for every people who discovered its secret. With iron-pointed spears, a people could hunt more effectively than their neighbors who had only stone or bronze weapons. They could defend themselves from wild animals better. Iron tools meant more food. People could clear land and raise crops more easily with iron axes and hoes.
>
> During Africa's early history, populations grew large in West Africa. The soil of the savanna was fertile and could provide food for increasing numbers of people. The people could settle in large, permanent communities. Travel on the savanna was also easier.

Figure 3–2 Sixth grade social studies text. From *The World Past and Present*, p. 266. Copyright 1985 by Harcourt Brace Jovanovich. Dale-Chall readability of full text = 7–8th grade; of passage = 7th grade.

These illustrations show how Bill's lag of about two years in reading achievement in grade 6 might influence negatively his learning in science, social studies, and other subject areas.

Results of Phonics and Fluency Assessments

We obtained two additional measures of reading—the students' knowledge of phonics and the fluency of their oral reading—which further illustrate the differences between above-average and below-average readers. The results of these measures, which did not lend themselves to grade equivalent conversions, are presented below.

Phonics. The phonics test was administered individually to each child and consisted of items designed to assess the fundamentals of phonic knowledge (consonant sounds, blends, and digraphs; short vowels, long vowels, vowel digraphs, and diphthongs; and the reading of polysyllabic words). Students could score up to 12 points for knowledge of the various phonic elements. Table 3-8 presents the results of the phonics test for each grade from 2 to 7 and for the above-average and below-average readers.

The results for phonics are significant for several reasons. First, each grade did quite well, reaching near maximum scores as early as grade 3. Second, as for other tests in the reading battery, the differences between the above-average and below-average readers in grades 2 and 3 are small, but the differences increase in grades 4 and

Table 3-8 Mean scores on phonic knowledge test for total group, above-average group, and below-average group, grades 2–7

Grade	Total group	Above-average group	Below-average group	Difference between above- and below-average groups
Grade 2	9.9	10.0	9.8	−.2
Grade 3	11.5	11.5	11.5	0
Gains from grade 2 to 3	+1.6	+1.5	+1.7	+.2
Grade 4	11.5	12.0	10.8	−1.2
Grade 5	11.8	12.0	11.6	−.4
Gains from grade 4 to 5	+.3	perfect scores	+.8	—
Grade 6	11.6	12.0	11.3	−.7
Grade 7	12.0	12.0	12.0	0
Gains from grade 6 to 7	+.4	perfect scores	+.7	—

6. All above-average readers reached perfect scores by grade 4; the below-average readers did not receive perfect scores until grade 7.

Fluency. Fluency refers to the ease, smoothness, and pace of a student's reading, particularly during oral reading of connected text. It has long been known to be an important aspect of reading development (Buswell, 1922). Indeed, current theories of the reading process as well as research confirm the importance of fluency for both silent reading comprehension and oral reading. If the reading of text is not fluent and automatic, comprehension suffers (LaBerge and Samuels, 1976; Stanovich, 1982; Chall, 1983b; Perfetti, 1985). We therefore investigated the reading fluency of our population and related it to their overall reading development.

To estimate fluency, we used the qualitative comments made by examiners during the child's oral reading of a passage that was on the student's instructional level (Table 3-9). Based on the examiner's comments, each pupil was rated as being either fluent or dysfluent. We then examined the fluency ratings by grade and for above-average and below-average readers (Table 3-10).

We found that two-thirds of the children in our sample were fluent.

Table 3-9 Oral reading qualities classified as fluent and dysfluent

Fluency (+)
- reads quickly without hesitation
- reads smoothly with natural delivery
- good word attack skills
- reads quickly, having problems only with "tricky" pronunciation
- attacks words without sounding them out

Disfluency (−)
- reads haltingly
- oversounds words
- reads word by word without inflection
- reads slowly
- tends to repeat words
- tends to ignore punctuation (e.g., runs through periods)
- uses finger for marking place

Table 3-10 Fluency ratings for above-average and below-average readers

Grade	No. of fluent students	No. of dysfluent students	Totals
Grades 2–3			
Above-average readers	4	0	4
Below-average readers	2	3	5
Grades 4–5			
Above-average readers	7	0	7
Below-average readers	2	3	5
Grades 6–7			
Above-average readers	4	0	4
Below-average readers	1	3	4
All grades			
Above-average readers	15	0	15
Below-average readers	5	9	14

However, we found considerable differences between the above-average and below-average readers: all of the above-average readers at each grade received fluent ratings, but no more than 40 percent of the below-average readers were rated fluent at any one grade. Thus, at grades 2 and 3 (when, theoretically, most readers begin to become fluent; see Chall, 1983b), all of the above-average readers were classified as fluent, but many of the below-average readers were rated as dysfluent. This pattern was evident through grade 7. Across grades, then, fluency seemed to characterize the reading of the above-average readers but not the below-average ones. Nor did the below-average readers seem to develop greater fluency with age. Indeed, our ratings indicate that the proportion of dysfluent to fluent readers in the below-average group was higher in grades 6 and 7 than it was in the earlier grades. This may indicate that the below-average readers had more serious reading problems than anticipated. Although we did not include students in stanine 1 in order to have a population without learning disabilities, we may well have inadvertently included some learning-disabled students.

Follow-up after Five Years

Twenty-six of the students were retested five years after the start of the study, when they were in grades 7, 9, and 11.* The seventh graders had been the second graders in our sample during the first year of the study; the ninth graders had been in fourth grade; and the eleventh graders had been in sixth grade. Since different tests of the students' reading were used in this follow-up, direct comparisons with the earlier test scores are not possible. However, we can compare the trends found for grades 7, 9, and 11 with those found for the earlier grades.

Reading Test Results

The patterns of test scores for the seventh, ninth, and eleventh grades were similar to those we found when the students were in the intermediate and upper elementary grades. On most tests the scores were below norms, and the discrepancies grew larger in each succeeding grade. By grade 11, the students' reading scores were considerably below norms, as low as the 25th percentile. When one recalls that in

*Irene Goodman and her colleagues, Wendy Barnes, Jean Chandler, and Lowry Hemphill, conducted the follow-up study and provided us with their data. A full report of these data can be found in the final chapter of *Unfulfilled Expectations* (Snow et al., in press).

grades 2 and 3 these children tested on grade level (that is, at about the 50th percentile, or within the norms) on similar tests, the extent of the deceleration by grade 11 is overwhelming.

As in the earlier grades, the pattern of deceleration varied on the different tests. The scores on the reading tests that did not permit the student to rely on context decelerated earlier and faster than the tests that permitted the use of context (reading comprehension). In grades 7 and 9, reading comprehension was the strongest when compared to the other reading tests; by grade 11, however, reading comprehension had also fallen—to the 25th percentile.

When the students were in elementary school, their scores on reading comprehension and oral reading tests also held up longer than their scores that did not rely on context (word meaning, spelling, word recognition)—probably because the students compensated for their lack of precise knowledge of word recognition and word meanings by relying on context. A similar scenario seems appropriate for the students in the seventh to eleventh grades. In grades 7 and 9 their relatively high scores on reading comprehension were possible as long as their word meaning and word recognition scores were not too low; they could compensate for moderately weak word recognition with their use of context. However, when there was too great a gap between the students' word recognition skills and the difficulty of the reading materials they were required to read, their ability to use context was no longer adequate to meet the demands.

As predicted by the model of reading development used in the study, different emphases in reading are needed at different times; and when they are lacking, later development will suffer. The trends in scores for the seventh to eleventh graders as well as the trends when they were younger suggest that we cannot be sanguine when the students do well in silent reading comprehension but have difficulty in word meaning and word recognition. These trends indicate that if the students are weak in word meanings, particularly in academic vocabularies, and in recognizing and spelling these less common words, they will decelerate later in reading comprehension. Both the original and the follow-up studies indicate that such problems do not go away; they ultimately erode strengths that students may have.

The low-income children in our study did not lack the ability to comprehend what they read (that is, to do higher-level analysis of what they read) as measured by the reading comprehension tests. The developmental history of these low-income students indicates that they could read with comprehension. Weaknesses were not found prior to grade 4; in grades 2 and 3 these students tested at grade level on all tests of reading and word meaning. What made these students fall behind around fourth grade was their slow acquisition of an academic vocabulary, their relative weakness in recognizing less familiar words, and their lack of fluency.

Why Do These Trends Occur?

How can one explain the trends we found: that through grades 2 and 3 the children's scores were on a par with a normative population—one that was composed of a representative mix of the population, including middle-class children—but at grade 4 and beyond their scores decelerated in comparison to the norm?

The general trend of decreasing gains with increasing grades is reminiscent of findings from other studies. The landmark study of Coleman and his associates (1966) found both that the verbal achievement of children from lower-income families was lower than that for the general population and that the discrepancies increased with increasing years in school. The National Assessments of Educational Progress for reading from 1971 to 1986 report the same trends: while the typical disadvantaged urban students at age 9 are about one year below the overall national average, they are four to five years behind at age 17 (Applebee, Langer, and Mullis, 1988).

One explanation for the increasing deceleration with increasing years in school comes from the developmental model of reading that was the theoretical base for the present study (Chall, 1979, 1983b). For the purpose of the present analysis, it is helpful to divide Chall's six stages of reading into two major categories—Stages 0, 1, and 2 (beginning reading, grades kindergarten through third) and Stages 3, 4, and 5 ("mature reading," grade 4 through college). Essentially, the major learning task for reading in kindergarten through grade 3 is recognition and decoding of words seen in print—words that the children already know when they are heard or spoken. Typically, children can use and comprehend when heard about 5,000 or 6,000 words when they enter grade 1; but it takes most children about three years to recognize them in print. It is significant that most children in the primary grades (1 to 3), even those with limited English, are more advanced in language and thinking than in reading skills. Therefore, the main task of reading instruction in the early grades is to teach the children to recognize words they already know. Children learn letters, their sounds, and the relationships between them, and they learn to recognize whole words and practice using these in the reading of stories, poems, and other connected texts for comprehension and pleasure. As accuracy and speed of word recognition develop, fluency also develops.

The fact that, in grades 2 and 3, our sample of low-SES children scored on grade level on the tests of word recognition, oral reading, and spelling indicates that they were making good progress in these beginning reading tasks. These skills are usually learned in school, and the school did indeed provide a strong instructional program in beginning reading for most of these children.

These children were also on grade level in word meaning when they were in the second and third grades. The words they were asked to define in these grades were, in general, common, familiar, concrete words. When asked to define these words, the low-SES children did as well or better than other children in the same grade. This is of particular importance because various language theories have attributed the low literacy achievement of poor children to language deficiencies or differences originating in preschool. Although we found a slump in word meanings at about grade 4 and above, it is important to note that the low-SES children had the word knowledge that other children had when they were in grades 2 and 3. Thus, in both beginning reading skills and knowledge of word meanings, these students were on a par with the general population in the primary grades.

Reading Stages 3 to 5 (grade levels 4 through college) increasingly focus on the reading of unfamiliar texts and on the use of reading as a tool for learning. At these advanced stages the reading materials become more complex, technical, and abstract and are beyond the everyday experiences of most children. Beginning in about fourth grade, readers must cope with ever more complex demands upon language, cognition, and reading skills. Whereas the major hurdles prior to grade 4 are learning to recognize in print the thousands of words whose meanings are already known and reading these fluently in connected texts with comprehension, the hurdle of grade 4 and beyond is coping with increasingly complex language and thought. If students' word recognition, decoding, or fluency are weak, they will be unable to meet the demands of reading at the higher stages, even if they have good meaning vocabularies and can do higher-order thinking.

Why, then, do students with strong beginning reading and word meaning skills through grade 3 show a slip in scores beginning at about the fourth grade? First, as just discussed, the reading task changes around grade 4 from a focus on reading familiar texts where the task is one of recognizing and decoding words to one of comprehension of harder texts that use more difficult, abstract, specialized, and technical words. The concepts used in textbooks also become more abstract, and understanding them requires more sophisticated levels of background knowledge and cognition. In addition, fourth-grade students are expected to begin to use reading as a tool for learning and analyzing new ideas, facts, and opinions. Thus, the transition from the reading task of the primary grades to that of the intermediate grades requires more knowledge of word meanings, and requires more advanced word recognition, greater facility in decoding, and greater fluency in reading printed text, in order to make a shift from concentrating on the recognition of words to concentrating on meanings and ideas. This is perhaps one of the most important transitions made in reading, and difficulties in making it have long been known (Orton, 1937; LaBerge and Samuels, 1976; Chall, 1983b). Although the above-average readers could make the transition in grade 4, the below-average fourth graders did not seem to be able to do so.

What Factors Affect the Slump?

Students seem to need two kinds of strengths in order to avoid the fourth-grade slump: a sufficient knowledge of the meanings of more academic and abstract words, and a facility with advanced word recognition, spelling, and fluency. Thus, at grade 4, the below-average readers who were behind in both knowledge of word meanings and word recognition experienced the earlier and more intensive decelerations. The above-average readers' course of development was different. Like the below-average readers, they had fallen below national norms on word meanings in the fourth grade; but, unlike the below-average group, they remained strong in word recognition, spelling, and fluency. Thus, it may be hypothesized that the above-average readers were able to compensate for their weakness in word meanings with their strong skills in word recognition and fluency. These factors help to explain the early and intense slip in grade 4 shown by the below-average readers, in contrast to the above-average readers, whose deceleration on most reading tests came later and with less intensity.

The higher scores of both the above-average and below-average readers on contextualized tasks (silent reading comprehension and oral reading) as compared to decontextualized tasks (word meaning, word recognition, and spelling) suggest that these students have adequate cognition and comprehension. They seem, however, to be weaker in the reading-specific tasks of word recognition and fluency—which, in time, limits their abilities with reading comprehension and other tasks that require more cognitive abilities. Tables 3-11 and 3-12 show the differences in scores on contextual versus decontextualized tests among both groups of readers in our sample. These tables show clearly that the children scored higher, at each grade, on tasks that required the use of context and scored lower on those tests that required using words out of context. This was true for both the above-average and below-average readers.

Our findings and interpretations tend to run counter to those of the National Assessment of Educational Progress, which interprets the slippage in reading scores at higher levels as stemming from deficiencies in higher-level comprehension skills, and to other current views on the major importance of cognition in reading development (see also Anderson et al., 1985; Curtis, 1986; Applebee, Langer, and Mullis, 1987; Chall, 1989a).

Correlational and Exploratory Factor Analyses

Correlational Analysis

To gain further insights into the broad factors that accounted for the reading development of our students, we intercorrelated the six tests in the reading battery. Table 3-13 presents the number of significant correlations among the reading components out of a total of nine possible. We found the highest correlations among the tests that measured aspects of word recognition (word recognition, spelling, phonics, and oral reading). Thus, the word recognition scores were highly related to phonics, oral reading, and spelling; oral reading, in turn, was highly related to phonics and spelling; and spelling was highly related to phonics.

Correlations for the separate grades also revealed that the word meaning scores had the lowest correlations with the print-related reading tests in grades 2 through 5. However, at grades 6 and 7, the word meaning scores correlated highly with the various reading measures, particularly with silent reading comprehension—suggesting the increasing importance of word meanings as the reading materials become more difficult.

In the early grades, word meaning scores had lower correlations

Table 3-11 Mean test scores on contextualized and decontextualized tasks, above-average and below-average readers, grades 2, 4, and 6

	Above-average readers			Below-average readers		
	Decontextualized	Contextualized	Difference	Decontextualized	Contextualized	Difference
Grade 2	2.8	3.1	+.3	2.9	3.2	+.3
Grade 4	4.9	5.9	+1.0	3.9	4.3	+.4
Grade 6	6.3	7.4	+1.1	4.8	6.0	+1.2

Table 3-12 Mean test scores on contextualized and decontextualized tasks, above-average and below-average readers, grades 3, 5, and 7

	Above-average readers			Below-average readers		
	Decontextualized	Contextualized	Difference	Decontextualized	Contextualized	Difference
Grade 3	4.0	5.0	+1.0	4.0	5.0	+1.0
Grade 5	6.2	8.0	+1.8	5.0	5.4	+.4
Grade 7	7.2	8.7	+1.5	5.5	6.6	+1.1

Table 3-13 Correlations among reading components across grades

Reading components	Number of significant correlations
Word recognition/oral reading	+7/9
Word recognition/word meaning	+0/9
Word recognition/silent reading	+4/9
Word recognition/spelling	+4/7
Word recognition/phonics	+6/9
Oral reading/word meaning	+3/9
Oral reading/silent reading	+5/9
Oral reading/spelling	+7/9
Oral reading/phonics	+7/9
Word meaning/spelling	+0/9
Word meaning/phonics	+5/9
Silent reading/spelling	+5/9
Silent reading/phonics	+7/9
Spelling/phonics	+8/9

with reading than did word recognition and phonics. These correlations confirm the results of research over nearly seven decades that word recognition and phonics are of first importance for progress in early reading (Chall, 1967, 1983a; Perfetti, 1985; Williams, 1986; Ehri, 1987; Juel, 1988). Beyond the primary grades, word meanings and comprehension are more highly correlated. (See E. L. Thorndike, 1917; Davis, 1972; R. L. Thorndike, 1973–74; Chall and Stahl, 1985.)

Factor Analysis

We performed exploratory factor analyses to gain further evidence on the relationships between word meaning and the different reading tests for the total population and separately for each grade. A factor analysis can indicate common factors running through the various tests and the potency of these factors; "loadings" indicate the strengths of various tests on a given factor. Table 3-14 presents the results for the entire population. One factor—a general reading factor—had high loadings from all the reading tests except word meaning. Word meaning could be considered a second factor. Thus, in the factor analysis the tests grouped themselves the same way they did in

Table 3-14 Factor loadings for total population

Reading component	Factor loadings of pretest scores (grades 2, 4, and 6 combined)	Factor loadings of posttest scores (grades 3, 5, and 7 combined)
Word recognition	.91	.93
Oral reading	.93	.89
Word meaning	.62	.46
Silent reading	.94	.82
Spelling	.82	.87
Phonics	.83	.60[a]

a. The lower score can be attributed to a ceiling effect.

the correlational analyses—the print-based tests were grouped together and were somewhat separate from the "nonreading" word meaning test.

We also performed a separate factor analysis for grades 2, 4, and 6 (Table 3-15). For grades 2 and 4 the results are similar to those found for the total population—a general reading factor with high loadings on all the reading tests except for word meaning. At grade 6 two different factors emerged. The first was a word meaning factor, with high loadings from word meaning, silent reading comprehension, and phonics; the second was a word recognition factor, with high loadings from word recognition, spelling, and oral reading.

Thus, the factor analyses found (as did the correlational analyses) that there were two components in the reading of our students—word recognition and word meaning.

A Scenario for the Cumulative Deficits

What is the best explanation for the pattern of reading development that we found among these children—the good start in the primary grades and the slump in the intermediate and higher grades? It should be recalled that the low-income children in our study were in the middle range of reading ability—half at stanines 2 and 3 (the below-average readers) and half at stanines 5 and 6 (the above-average readers). We did not include children in stanine 1, who might have serious reading problems or learning disabilities; we did not include those who were not proficient in English; and we did not

Table 3-15 Factor analyses of reading test scores, grades 2, 4, and 6

Grade and reading component	Total scores	
	F1	F2
Grade 2		
Word recognition	.67	
Oral reading	.85	
Word meaning	.56	
Silent reading	.95	
Spelling	.74	
Phonics	.85	
Grade 4		
Word recognition	.93	
Oral reading	.93	
Word meaning	−.42	
Silent reading	.74	
Spelling	.80	
Phonics	.88	
Grade 6		
Word recognition	.38	.77
Oral reading	.58	.77
Word meaning	.94	.07
Silent reading	.88	.20
Spelling	−.05	.72
Phonics	.89	.27

include children in stanines 7, 8, and 9 in order not to bias the sample toward exceptionally able children.

Our explanation for the trend in their achievement is based on two theoretical views: Carroll's view (1977) that reading comprehension depends on three major factors—language, cognition, and reading skills; and Chall's theory of stages of reading development (1979, 1983b), which views reading as going through a series of qualitative changes as it develops. The scenario presented below views the stages of reading in terms of Carroll's three factors—language, cognition, and reading skills.

At Stages 1 and 2 (grades 1–3), the reading skills of word recognition, decoding, and fluency are particularly important for reading achievement. Although language and cognition are also important in the earliest stages of reading, they seem to have less importance than word recognition and decoding. (See Perfetti, 1985; Stanovich, 1986; Freebody and Byrne, 1988; Chall, 1989b.) Reading comprehension in the early grades correlates higher with word recognition and phonics than with word meanings. For example, in kindergarten the highest correlation with reading is knowledge of the names of the letters of the alphabet. High correlations with early reading achievement have been found also for rhyming, sound discrimination, word segmentation, and auditory blending, all highly related to phonics and word recognition. Thus, in the earliest grades, word recognition and phonics are the critical skills for success with the reading tasks and materials typical of these grades.

A general shift takes place at about grade 4, when language and cognition become the stronger predictors of reading—a time also when the curriculum begins to include systematic formal study of science, social studies, and literature. The textbooks and other instructional materials reflect this change, containing more difficult concepts, vocabulary, syntax, and organization. The reading tests reflect these changes as well (Auerbach, 1971). From fourth grade through high school, the research literature generally indicates higher and stronger correlations of reading with cognition and language than with word recognition and phonics.

Judging from their scores in grades 2 and 3, we can hypothesize that our population of low-income children had the cognitive and linguistic abilities to learn to read. In these grades their performance was equal to national norms, and there were few differences between the good and the poor readers, except in fluency—with the below-average readers behind the above-average.

The students in our population were exposed to a strong beginning reading program in the primary grades; this was confirmed by their reading supervisors and teachers. During the study most children were taught with a basal reading series and correlated workbooks. In addition, the younger students used a separate phonics workbook. Library books were also available in classrooms for independent reading.

At about grade 4, when the curriculum requires higher cognitive and linguistic performance, the children's reading began to slip. They slumped first on word meanings, particularly on abstract, literary, less common words. The next drop was in word recognition and spelling, also on less common, low-frequency words. The lower scores in word recognition and spelling could also have been influenced by the lower scores in word meanings, for when the meanings of words are not known, they are harder to identify and spell. The last, and lowest, relative decline was in oral reading and silent reading comprehension—tasks that provided the students with contexts and permitted intelligent guessing.

A key question is why the above-average and below-average readers who were both on grade level in grades 2 and 3 began to pull apart in grade 4 and grow further apart in grades 5 to 7. In the primary grades, both groups had similar strengths in language, cognition, and reading skills. In the intermediate grades, both slumped at about the same time and with about equal intensity on word meanings. They differed, however, in oral and silent reading: the above-average readers stayed on grade level or above until about grade 6, while the below-average readers were already testing below grade level in grade 4. We offer the following as a likely explanation.

Although knowledge of word meanings is essential in the intermediate grades and higher, it is possible when the reading tasks provide context (as in oral and silent reading tests) for students to make intelligent guesses from the context. The above-average readers could do this better than the below-average readers in grades 4 to 7 because they had two strengths to help them—greater strengths in word recognition and in fluency. Although they were not superior to the below-average readers in word meanings, their greater abilities in identifying longer and harder words and their greater fluency in reading connected texts resulted in their higher performance when reading such texts.

It is possible that, through grade 6 or 7, accurate recognition, decoding, and fluency can make up for a lack of precise word knowledge, especially on the oral and silent reading tests, which allow students the chance to use their cognitive abilities to guess from context. However, at sixth or seventh grade and beyond, skill in word meaning becomes increasingly crucial.

Why would low-income children decelerate first and most intensively in word meanings? The words they did not know were the less familiar, less common words usually acquired through being read to, through a student's own wide reading, through the study of the various content subjects, and through direct instruction. Although we did not compare our population with a middle-class group of the same age, one could speculate that our population probably owned and read fewer books (see NAEP, 1985); and they may have been read to less than middle-class children (Chomsky, 1972).

Thus, it would appear that the linguistic and literacy environment of our population was sufficient for their reading achievement in the primary grades but not for their reading in the intermediate and upper elementary grades. We discuss the literacy environments of these students at home and in school in Chapters 7 and 8.

4

Writing Development

We now know that deceleration in reading development occurred for most of the children in our sample. But does this slump occur for writing as well? What trends in writing development emerged in grades 2 through 7? Was the writing of the children relatively stronger in some grades than in others? Were the above-average readers better writers than the below-average readers?

In analyzing the writing development of the children, we were faced with a different sort of problem—what measures to use. In contrast to reading, there has been little agreement about the best ways to assess writing. Therefore, we used many different techniques to analyze the essays written by the children: holistic ratings; scaled assessments of form, content, organization, and handwriting; and counts of total production, syntax, vocabulary, and spelling errors. This chapter begins with an overview of our methods and findings, with general observations on the meaning of the results; we then present descriptions and analysis of all the measures and the results, with more specific implications for practice.

General Findings

As in our analysis of reading, we studied the course of development in writing for children in grades 2, 4, and 6 and a year later when they were in grades 3, 5, and 7. We also compared the writing of the above-average and below-average readers on both the narrative and expository essays.

As with reading, we found a deceleration in writing development for the children in our sample. In general, the scores on most writing measures increased considerably up to grade 4 or 5, but the scores for students in grades 6 and 7 were only slightly higher than those for grades 4 and 5. This was found in both narration and exposition, and it was consistent across most of the three types of measures we used. Deceleration was especially salient in the holistic ratings (which examine the overall goodness and maturity of writing) and production (the number of words written on each stimulus in ten minutes).

Although some variations were linked to the genre of writing (narration versus exposition), on most measures the course of development was similar. The writing of the grade 2–3 students was characterized by short sentences, unconnected lists of statements, the use of only the most common vocabulary, and very limited production. Punctuation, capitalization, and spelling showed little accuracy. Thus, the writing of the grade 2–3 students reflected a struggle to master the very simplest forms of writing. In contrast, the grade 4–5 students demonstrated greater maturity, precision, and production than that of the younger children. Fourth and fifth grade discourse was more connected and developed than that of the second and third graders; the older students showed greater ability to get their ideas on paper (production). However, they still had difficulty with form and mechanics, and their vocabulary was still limited to very common words.

The writing of the grade 6–7 students was not much different from that of the grade 4–5 students. The older children were a little better at writing connected discourse; they were less apt to produce a series of loosely connected facts. But in many ways they demonstrated the same difficulties as the grade 4–5 children: they showed weaknesses in spelling and punctuation, and their usage of vocabulary was still very limited.

Our analysis yielded similar results for both above-average and below-average readers—considerable gains from the primary grades (2–3) to the middle grades (4–5), but much slower development from the middle grades to the upper grades (6–7).

As the detailed analysis in the next section shows, the decelerative pattern in writing development repeats itself across most measures. Children made good progress from the primary to the middle grades (on all measures), but after grade 4 or 5 their writing development slowed.

The Writing Samples

Writing samples were used to map the development of the children's writing ability in the same way as reading test data were used to map their reading ability. We used the writing samples to determine the course of development of the children's writing ability on both narration and exposition, from grades 2 through 7. We compared the writing of the above-average and below-average readers to determine the relative strengths and weaknesses in writing of each group. We also studied relationships between the children's writing ability and their abilities in reading and language.

The Writing Stimuli and Data Collection

When the study was designed, few standardized writing measures had been developed (see Myklebust, 1965; Hammill and Larsen, 1978; compare Fagan, Cooper, and Jensen, 1975; Cooper and Odell, 1977). There was some evidence, however, that different genres of writing (for example, description, narration, argumentation, and explanation) place different demands on a writer. After considering many possible kinds of writing stimuli, we decided to use two kinds: narrative and expository. The two writing stimuli we chose had been used by the National Assessment of Educational Progress (NAEP, 1971). Two similar writing assessments, used experimentally at the Harvard Reading Laboratory to diagnose the writing of elementary and high school students, had been found useful.

The narrative stimulus was a picture of an elderly woman holding a package of tomatoes (Figure 4-1). The instructions to the subjects were the same as those used by the NAEP:

> Here is a picture of a woman with some tomatoes. Look at the picture for a while and think about what is going on. When you have decided, write a story that tells what is happening in the picture and what is likely to happen next.

The directions for the expository stimulus were adapted from those used by the NAEP:

> Many of us have a special person whom we look up to or admire for reasons that are very special to us. For example, some people admire or look up to famous sports players, to TV or movie stars, to a person in a story, or to a relative or friend. Write about whom you admire or look up to; tell who the person is and explain why you look up to this person.

Each child completed a narrative and an expository sample in May or June of the first year of the study (when the subjects were completing grades 2, 4, or 6) and again in April or May of the second year (when subjects were completing grades 3, 5, or 7). The children completed the samples under individual supervision in a quiet room apart

Figure 4–1 Narrative stimulus for the writing sample.

from their regular classroom. The students were given ten minutes to complete each writing task.

Assessment of the Samples

In choosing the methods to analyze the writing samples, we were sensitive to the fact that assessment, at the time of the study, was in a state of flux. Prior to the 1970s, the focus of writing assessment had been on the written product and on the measurement of skill in such discrete aspects of writing as spelling, handwriting, and grammatical usage. During the late 1970s and early 1980s research interests turned toward the processes by which writers produced meaningful prose (for example, Flower and Hayes, 1980; Bereiter and Scardamalia, 1982). These researchers assumed that the written product was greater than the sum of its discrete parts and asserted that good writing assessment must include some measure of the process by which the writing was produced or the meaning-making aspect of composing that "glues" a piece together.

At about the same time that research turned to investigating the writing process, the Educational Testing Service (ETS) began to use holistic evaluation to gauge the overall goodness or maturity of writing produced on its various College Board measures (Fowles, 1978). One premise of holistic evaluation is that the whole of a piece of writing is greater than the sum of its parts and that a paper's goodness or maturity is best judged relative to other papers in a particular sample. Since its introduction, holistic scoring has been used on national, state, and local levels in large-scale assessments of writing and has also been adapted in the classroom for guided instruction.

We studied the literature for assessment procedures that would represent the best of those available and that would also yield generalizable information.* For example, we benefited from Myklebust (1965), who in his assessment of writing included measures of production (total words, sentences, and words per sentence), syntax (word usage, order, and punctuation), and meaning (represented by a rating of 1 to 5 that measured the continuum of complexity of meaning—from meaningless language to abstract-imaginative language). We also learned from Hammill and Larsen's *Test of Written Language* (1978)—one of the few standardized tests of composition—which included both objective and "spontaneous" measures of mechanics (handwriting), conventions (punctuation), linguistics (syntax, semantics, and style), and cognition (logic, coherence, and sequence). We were also influenced by the ETS evaluation procedures, which used holistic measures (as described above) and analytic trait scoring (which assumes that the written product is the sum of separable aspects which can each be assessed and that "correctness" can be measured against criteria from outside the paper itself; see Diederich, 1974; Cooper and Odell, 1977; Fowles, 1978).

Based on our study of the available assessment procedures for writing, we chose three different modes of measurement: holistic, analytic, and quantitative.

1. *Holistic Scoring*. Three proficient adult writers were trained in methods of holistic scoring according to the guidelines provided by ETS (Fowles, 1978). They then rated the narrative samples against one another for their overall maturity on a four-point scale (1 for the least mature papers and 4 for the most mature papers). Each paper was also ranked from 1 to 30—from the least mature to the most mature

*We did not use protocol analysis—a process by which writers explain how they are writing while they are composing. Protocol analyses are essentially case studies, which can be useful in research or in a teacher's understanding of one student's writing process, but which are rarely generalizable to larger populations.

paper in the sample. The process was repeated for the expository samples.

2. *Analytic Trait Scoring*. Three proficient adult writers were trained in methods of analytic trait scoring (see Diederich, 1974; Cooper and Odell, 1977; Fowles, 1978). The raters then evaluated specific aspects of each child's writing against criteria outside of the realm of the papers. Specifically, the raters examined the following aspects of writing according to the following scales (1 represents the lowest rating and 3 or 4 represents the highest rating).

Content rating (1 = lowest; 4 = highest):

1 = no "story"; one sentence or two unconnected sentences.

2 = a flat list of facts or details.

3 = an interesting, varied presentation, developed primarily through enumeration of fact with some explicit connection made between facts.

4 = an interesting, varied presentation, developed logically with such strategies as cause and effect, illustration, example, or detail.

Form rating (1 = lowest; 4 = highest):

1 = severe sentence-structure problems (for example, fragmentation) as well as severe grammatical and mechanical problems.

2 = sentence-structure problems (for example, run-ons) coupled with other grammatical and mechanical problems.

3 = a few isolated errors in mechanics and sentence structure; grammar is largely correct.

4 = no errors or perhaps one or two isolated errors.

Organization rating (1 = lowest; 3 = highest):

1 = incoherent writing; no obvious connections between thoughts and/or utterances.

2 = listing of ideas; little or no connective design.

3 = organized writing; clear and purposeful design.

Handwriting rating (1 = lowest; 3 = highest):

1 = illegible handwriting, characterized by inconsistent spacing and irregularly shaped letters.

2 = legible handwriting.

3 = neat, stylized handwriting.

3. *Quantitative Measures*

Production: the total number of words produced in each sample.

Syntax:

Average T-unit length: The number of words produced per sample divided by the total number of T-units (defined as "one main clause plus the subordinate clauses attached to or embedded within it") produced for that sample (Hunt, 1965, p. 49).

Average utterance length: The average length of what appeared to be a "sensical" sentence regardless of the punctuation and/or capitalization used. (Unlike T-units, utterances could be compound sentences.)

Vocabulary:

Average number of words not on the *1,000 Common Words* used in the *Spache Formula* (Spache, 1974).

Average number of words not on the *Dale List of 3,000 Words* (familiar to fourth graders; Dale and Chall, 1948).

Spelling: The percentage of misspelled words (total number of misspelled words divided by the total number of words written).

Results of the Writing Assessments

The results of these various assessments were analyzed for trends by grade and by above-average and below-average readers in four categories: (1) overall measures (holistic rating, holistic ranking, and production); (2) syntactic-organizational measures (organization rating, T-unit length, and sentence/utterance length); (3) content measures (content rating and unfamiliar Spache and Dale vocabulary); and (4) precision measures (form rating, percentage of misspelled words, and handwriting).

The different measures that we used in the study produced some variation in the developmental trends that emerged for grades 2 through 7. There was also variation according to genre (whether the writing was narrative or expository) and according to whether a student was an above-average or a below-average reader. Despite these variations, however, one trend emerged more often than others—a kind of decelerative trend. In general, scores on writing measures seemed to increase through grades 4 or 5. But the scores of students in grades 6 and 7 were only slightly higher or were lower than those of students in grades 4 or 5; thus the gains decelerated in the later grades. This is the same trend we found for reading.

Findings from Overall Measures

The decelerative trend we found in the students' writing can be seen in their scores on both narration and exposition on the two most general measures of writing: holistic rating and production.* Table 4-1 presents the mean holistic rating and production on narration for each grade that we tested: grades 2 (and grade 3 when these students were retested a year later), 4 (and grade 5 at retesting), and 6 (and grade 7 at retesting). The table also shows a piece of student writing that most closely represents students' mean rating and production at each grade, 2 through 7. (Appendix A shows these same samples in the students' own handwriting.)

It can be seen from Table 4-1 that the holistic ratings for narration increase at each grade. However, while the grade 4–5 students' ratings are much stronger than those of the grade 2–3 students (about 1 to 1.5 points higher), the grade 6–7 students' ratings are only slightly stronger than those of the grade 4–5 students (no more than about 0.5 point higher). This decelerative trend is even more obvious for production: the grade 4–5 students' papers are much longer than those of the grade 2–3 students (about two to three times longer), but the grade 6–7 students' papers are about the same length, if not shorter, than those of the grade 4–5 students.

A look at the students' writing reveals that the grade 2–3 students produced the shortest and least mature writing; their ratings never averaged above 2.0 (out of 4.0). They produced only the shortest of sentences, and they presented them in an unconnected way, in the form of a list. The youngest students demonstrated little skill in the more precise aspects of writing, such as punctuation, capitalization, and spelling.

The writing of the grade 4–5 students was much stronger than the grade 2–3 writing; it is rated in the high 2.0 range. These students wrote longer and syntactically more complex sentences, and their narratives told more of a connected story, although they did continue to rely on a list-like presentation. The grade 4–5 students demonstrated a better understanding of the precise aspects of writing than did the students in grades 2–3; however, their writing still reflected problems with form and mechanics.

The writing of the grade 6–7 students was not much different from that of the grade 4–5 students; it was rated in the high 2.0 or low 3.0

*Because the holistic rankings correlated so highly with the holistic ratings (.94), we report only the holistic ratings in the present analysis.

range. The grade 6–7 students told more of a connected story than the grade 4–5 students; they seemed to rely less on list-like, additive presentations and more on cause and effect. However, their writing still manifested the same problems with precision in spelling and punctuation that the grade 4–5 students manifested.

Table 4-2 presents the mean holistic rating and production on exposition for grades 2 through 7; it also shows a sample of student writing that most closely represents students' mean expository rating and production at each grade. (Appendix B shows these samples in the students' own handwriting.) The table shows that trends in expository ratings and production are similar to those on narration: that is, greater differences in ratings and production are found between grades 2–3 and 4–5 than between grades 4–5 and 6–7.

Comparison of Above-Average and Below-Average Readers

The course of development among the above-average and below-average readers on the overall measures of holistic rating and production for both narration and exposition was essentially the same as for the entire sample of students: both groups of readers exhibited a decelerative trend in their writing. Table 4-3 presents the mean holistic scores for above-average and below-average readers at grades 2 through 7 on narration and exposition; it also presents the students' mean production. The above-average readers' mean holistic ratings and production clearly illustrate the decelerative trend already described for the entire sample. The above-average readers in grades 4–5 wrote much longer narrations and expositions (two to three times longer), which were rated much higher (at least 1.5 points higher) than those of the above-average readers in grades 2–3. The above-average readers in grades 6–7, however, produced narrations and expositions that were more similar to than different from those of the grade 4–5 above-average readers: their papers were about the same length (or slightly shorter) and were rated only about a half-point higher than those of the grade 4–5 above-average readers.

On narration and exposition, the below-average readers exhibit trends similar to those of the above-average ones. Table 4-3 shows that the below-average readers in grades 4–5 wrote much longer narrations and expositions than did the below-average readers in grades 2–3 (up to two to three times longer), and their narrations and expositions were rated about a full point higher than those in grades 2–3. However, the narrations and expositions of the below-average grade 6–7 readers were about the same length or shorter than those of the

Table 4-1 Narrative writing at grades 2–7 on overall measures (mean holistic ratings and mean production)

Grade	Mean holistic rating (1 low to 4 high)	Mean production (number of words written)	Examples of writing[a]
2	1.2	23.3	ALN1 (holistic rating = 1.3; production = 25.0 words) Shes going to open it Shes holding it up Shes at a store and shes going to buy it Shes going home and eating it
3	1.6	40.1	PJN2 (holistic rating = 1.8; production = 24.0 words) The woman has some tomatoes. and she is looking at somone to throe them at. there are three tomatoes coverd with a plastic sheet. the old woman has glasses and a string of pearls. and a new dress. with stars on them.
4	2.6	69.2	KBN1 (holistic rating = 2.5; production = 74.0 words) This old lady has bot some tomatoes. And the store man thinks she stool them. He has called the police. And the old lady is very fritend. And soon the police cones. And ask here a lot of things like were did she get the tomatoes, what is her name, where do she liv. And she answerd all of then ersept for two and thay ware were she liv and what her name was.

5	2.7	86.9	AJN2 (holistic rating = 2.8; production = 96.0 words) This is an old lady looking for some big red juicy tomatoe's. she is going to bye some tomatoes. She when she get's home she might make salad to eat for lunch, she also might be Picking up some tomatoe's for here son's wife or a freind. After maybe a week after she will go back and get some more juicy tomatoes to eat or maybe lettuce this time. She might not even get vegativbles anymore She might get some nice lene meat. and have a cook out and have meat, coke, hamburgers, hotdogs and fruit Punch.
6	2.9	45.8	RMN1 (holistic rating = 2.8; production = 50.0 words) This is a woman that is going to buy some tomatoes. She is looking back to see if anybody is coming. So she can grab alot becaus they are on sale, and the are ripe and big. If she don't get any now she will never get them agan. the end
7	3.3	80.6	CTN2 (holistic rating = 3.0; production = 79.0 words) This is a picture of a old lady who is about to buy some tomatoes but she yelling and screaming about how expensive they are so she standing there wondering if she should buy or not so she decided to buy the tomatoes olny for half price but if she did that she would not be aloud in that particular store anymore. So she went along with the idea of not being able to go in the store anymore.

a. Note that these typed examples of students' writing are uncorrected; compare typed versions with handwritten versions in Appendix A. (The reproductions of the handwritten samples have been reduced to about 60 percent of full size.)

Table 4-2 Expository writing at grades 2–7 on overall measures (mean holistic ratings and mean production)

Grade	Mean holistic rating (1 low to 4 high)	Mean production (number of words written)	Examples of writing[a]
2	1.5	24.4	JFE1 (holistic rating = 1.5; production = 25.0 words) I admire my Farther cose wen um Faling bad makes me Fale Better and he's a good persing he buys me stuf like a bike
3	1.5	43.5	MHE2 (holistic rating = 1.3; production = 42.0 words) The Boston red sox are my favret bassball players the best one I like is jim rise I like how he hit's tose home run's and I like cow itscemkey and he hit's home run's to but the best one is me
4	2.8	64.6	BKE1 (holistic rating = 3.0; production = 70.0 words) I looke up to my mother and my farther because are the ones that beat all those T.V. Stars the story book people. and the sports people. And you can trust them with out a dout and if they gave me some thing thay wo'nt be ersepthig any thing back from me. I really don't know what that word means. but what they do for me I rally admire them for

5	2.8	94.3	GFE2 (holistic rating = 3.3; production = 95.0 words) I admire my carisin becase when ever i'm introble she sticks up for me. My causins name is X-X- She realy gets me out of trouble most of the time. and when ever I pick kids she tells me not to pick on then why don't you pick on some one your one size. thats how come I admire cosin. Thats how come I stick a round with her. ome tine when we were at X-- park I kept throaring pemies at people she said you betere stop it or were going home. and I would stop.
6	3.4	50.6	DWE1 (holistic rating = 3.3; production = 50.0 words) I look up to my friend X-X- she is very smart and she is friendly. I like her family there are nice espiecialy her grandmother she nice to me and my family. she always has alot of ideas that make sences that why I look up to her.
7	3.0	84.9	TCE2 (holistic rating = 3.0; production = 74.0 words) The person that I admire is a good friend of mine she has long black hair and is very pretty. she's very nice we do alot of things together. We always have fun were ever we go like when we go to the movies or saturday night with a couple of other people. But the really only other reason why I like X is because we never fight like me and my other friends.

a. Note that these typed examples of students' writing are uncorrected; compare typed version with handwritten versions in Appendix B. (The reproductions of the handwritten samples have been reduced to about 60 percent of full size.)

Table 4-3 Production and holistic ratings for above-average and below-average readers, grades 2 to 7

Production—Narration						
	Grade					
	2	3	4	5	6	7
Above-average	30.3	37.5	75.7	95.9	54.0	73.3
Below-average	18.7	41.8	60.0	74.4	37.5	88.0

Production—Exposition						
	Grade					
	2	3	4	5	6	7
Above-average	31.8	39.5	69.7	102.0	66.0	96.8
Below-average	19.5	46.2	57.4	83.4	35.3	73.0

Holistic Rating (1-4)—Narration						
	Grade					
	2	3	4	5	6	7
Above-average	1.3	1.5	3.0	2.8	3.3	3.3
Below-average	1.2	1.6	2.1	2.5	2.4	3.2

Holistic Rating (1-4)—Exposition						
	Grade					
	2	3	4	5	6	7
Above-average	1.7	1.3	3.1	3.0	3.7	3.4
Below-average	1.4	1.6	2.5	2.6	2.9	2.6

grade 4–5 students, and their papers were rated either about the same or, at most, a half-point higher.

We also compared the above-average and below-average readers' performance on the overall measures of the holistic score and production. On narration, the above-average and below-average readers received approximately the same ratings and wrote papers of about the same length in grades 2–3. Although the above-average readers' gains were greater at grades 4–5 than were those of the below-average readers, the below-average group seemed to catch up to the above-average readers by grade 7—when they again received similar ratings and produced papers of about the same length as the above-average group. On exposition, the above-average and below-average readers also received approximately the same ratings and wrote papers of about the same length in grades 2–3. However, in subsequent grades (4 through 7), the below-average readers consistently received lower ratings and wrote shorter papers than did the above-average readers. Thus, on exposition, the below-average group did not seem to catch up to the above-average group at grade 7, as they did on narration.

Findings from Syntactic-Organizational Measures

Table 4-4 presents the results for the measures of syntax (T-unit and utterance length) and text organization (a rating of goodness of organization from 1 to 3). The table includes scores for both the narrative and expository samples and the means for the total population as well as for the above-average and below-average readers.

Overall, the trend in the mean scores on syntactic-organizational measures for the total group is similar to the decelerative trend we found for the holistic ratings and production. The scores of the grade 4–5 students were generally much stronger than those for the grade 2–3 students; however, the scores of the grade 6–7 students were about the same—or only slightly higher or even lower—than those of the grade 4–5 students. We found this trend on both narration and exposition.

The above-average readers exhibited the same trend as did the total sample on both narrative and expository syntactic-organizational measures—that is, greater gains through about grades 4–5, then deceleration in gains in grades 6–7 (compared to grades 4–5). The below-average readers also exhibited decelerative trends. Most striking is the comparison between the above-average and the below-average readers' organizational ratings: the former group generally received higher organizational ratings than the latter after the earliest grades (4–7), especially for exposition.

Findings from Content and Precision Measures

Table 4-5 presents the results for the content measures (content rating and use of vocabulary unfamiliar to the Spache and Dale lists). The trends for two of the three content measures (content rating and vocabulary unfamiliar to the Spache list) are similar to those for the overall measures and the syntactic-organizational measures: decelera-

Table 4-4 Syntactic-organizational measures, grades 2 to 7

Average T-Unit Length (words)—Narration						
	Grade					
	2	3	4	5	6	7
Whole grade	8.3	10.4	10.0	12.3	9.9	11.8
Above-average	9.3	9.0	10.6	13.0	10.2	12.8
Below-average	7.5	11.3	9.1	11.4	9.6	10.8

Average T-Unit Length (words)—Exposition						
	Grade					
	2	3	4	5	6	7
Whole grade	7.6	8.9	11.3	11.2	9.3	10.7
Above-average	7.7	8.0	12.4	12.9	8.9	10.6
Below-average	7.6	9.5	9.8	8.9	9.6	10.8

Average Utterance Length (words)—Narration						
	Grade					
	2	3	4	5	6	7
Whole grade	8.7	11.4	10.7	14.7	13.2	15.1
Above-average	8.9	12.7	11.4	15.7	14.6	17.2
Below-average	8.5	10.5	9.8	13.2	11.8	13.0

tion in scores after grades 4–5. (There was too little use of vocabulary unfamiliar to the Dale list for us to observe much change among grades.) Thus, while grade 4–5 students made greater gains as compared to grade 2–3 students, those in grades 6–7 scored only slightly above those in grades 4–5.

Table 4-6 presents the results of the precision measures (form rating, misspelling, and handwriting). Two of the three precision measures (form rating and percentage of words misspelled) showed the same decelerative trend that we had already observed for the other measures. Handwriting generally continued to improve over grades.

The trends for the above-average and below-average readers on content and precision measures were similar to those for the total sample: that is, decelerative. Further, the above-average readers fared

Table 4-4 (continued)

Average Utterance Length (words)—Exposition						
	Grade					
	2	3	4	5	6	7
Whole grade	8.3	11.3	11.8	13.1	9.8	13.8
Above-average	8.7	9.2	12.7	14.7	10.0	14.3
Below-average	8.1	12.7	10.5	10.9	9.6	13.2

Organization Rating (1-3)—Narration						
	Grade					
	2	3	4	5	6	7
Whole grade	1.5	2.2	2.2	2.6	2.1	2.4
Above-average	1.5	2.3	2.3	2.6	2.3	2.5
Below-average	1.5	2.2	2.0	2.6	2.0	2.3

Organization Rating (1-3)—Exposition						
	Grade					
	2	3	4	5	6	7
Whole grade	1.9	2.0	2.0	2.2	2.4	2.3
Above-average	1.8	2.0	2.1	2.1	2.8	2.5
Below-average	2.0	2.0	1.8	2.2	2.0	2.0

consistently better than the below-average on precision measures in the later grades (4 through 7); this was true for both narration and exposition. On content measures, however, the below-average readers seemed to fare as well as the above-average in the later grades—especially on narration. Recall that, on overall measures, we also found a tendency for the below-average readers to perform as well as the above-average readers on narration.

Summary of Findings from Various Measures

In sum, for the broad categories—overall measures, syntactic-organizational measures, content measures, and precision measures—the developmental trends in students' writing were generally similar. We found greater differences between grade 2–3 and 4–5 performance

Table 4-5 Content measures, grades 2 to 7

Content Rating (1-4)—Narration						
	Grade					
	2	3	4	5	6	7
Whole grade	1.5	2.3	2.4	2.8	2.4	3.3
Above-average	1.8	2.4	2.7	2.9	2.8	3.3
Below-average	1.3	2.2	2.1	2.7	2.1	3.3
Content Rating (1-4)—Exposition						
	Grade					
	2	3	4	5	6	7
Whole grade	1.8	2.0	2.3	3.0	2.8	2.8
Above-average	1.8	1.9	2.4	3.0	3.0	3.2
Below-average	1.9	2.1	2.1	3.0	2.6	2.5
Percentage Unfamiliar Spache Words—Narration						
	Grade					
	2	3	4	5	6	7
Whole grade	6.4%	10.0%	6.5%	6.5%	9.3%	6.9%
Above-average	4.1%	11.2%	6.0%	6.8%	10.1%	7.2%
Below-average	7.9%	9.2%	7.1%	6.0%	8.0%	6.6%

than we did between grade 4–5 and 6–7 performance. The above-average readers generally fared better in writing than the below-average readers, especially on exposition. On narration, the below-average readers seemed to catch up to the above-average readers' performance on overall measures (holistic score and production) and on content ratings.

These trends were reminiscent of those we found for reading—greater gains in the earlier grades followed by decelerating gains. For most of the writing and reading measures, the deceleration starts after the primary grades; none of the measures start decelerating before grade 4. Although certain aspects of the children's writing do improve through grade 7—especially on narration and by the below-

Table 4-5 (continued)

Percentage Unfamiliar Spache Words—Exposition						
	Grade					
	2	3	4	5	6	7
Whole grade	5.1%	8.2%	6.4%	5.3%	6.7%	6.2%
Above-average	5.4%	8.7%	4.5%	5.9%	5.9%	4.0%
Below-average	4.8%	7.9%	9.2%	4.5%	7.5%	8.4%

Percentage Unfamiliar Dale Words—Narration						
	Grade					
	2	3	4	5	6	7
Whole grade	0.7%	1.8%	1.1%	0.9%	1.4%	0.8%
Above-average	0.0%	1.3%	1.2%	1.4%	2.2%	0.6%
Below-average	1.1%	2.1%	1.1%	0.3%	0.7%	0.9%

Percentage Unfamiliar Dale Words—Exposition						
	Grade					
	2	3	4	5	6	7
Whole grade	2.2%	3.5%	3.5%	2.6%	4.4%	3.0%
Above-average	2.9%	2.6%	2.8%	2.4%	3.6%	2.1%
Below-average	1.8%	4.2%	4.4%	2.8%	5.1%	3.9%

average readers—the trends for reading and writing are similar: faster development earlier, followed by increasingly smaller gains.

Weaknesses in Writing

Form versus Content

On reading and rereading the writing samples for the various analyses, we were struck by the discrepancies between the students' abilities to handle content and form. The students seemed to have good ideas, but they had difficulty with the grammar, mechanics, and spelling needed to express their ideas successfully in their writing. A comparison of the students' content and form ratings for narration

Table 4-6 Precision measures, grades 2 to 7

Form Rating (1-4)—Narration						
	Grade					
	2	3	4	5	6	7
Whole grade	1.4	1.9	1.9	2.0	2.3	2.3
Above-average	1.3	2.0	2.2	2.2	2.8	2.4
Below-average	1.5	1.8	1.4	1.6	1.7	2.1
Form Rating (1-4)—Exposition						
	Grade					
	2	3	4	5	6	7
Whole grade	1.1	1.3	1.5	1.9	1.9	2.1
Above-average	1.0	1.3	1.6	1.9	2.1	2.4
Below-average	1.2	1.4	1.3	1.9	1.8	1.8
Percentage of Words Misspelled—Narration						
	Grade					
	2	3	4	5	6	7
Whole grade	22.5%	6.5%	8.7%	7.9%	8.2%	8.9%
Above-average	23.5%	7.8%	6.1%	5.8%	5.3%	6.7%
Below-average	21.8%	5.6%	12.3%	10.8%	11.0%	11.0%

and exposition reveals the differences most pointedly. (See the outline of form and content ratings earlier in this chapter.) Table 4-7 presents the mean scores the students received on form and on content at grades 2 through 7 (the scores for narration and exposition have been combined). The table shows that the ratings for content are higher (by a half to a full point) than for form, grade for grade.

As dramatic as these quantitative differences between form and content are, the qualitative differences between the two are equally compelling. Table 4-8 presents examples of students' narrative writing at grades 3, 5, and 7 (the grades at which we might expect that each group of students would produce more mature writing). These samples received both content and form ratings that approximated the mean for their grade. To draw the reader's attention to the ideas being

Table 4-6 (continued)

Percentage of Words Misspelled—Exposition						
	Grade					
	2	3	4	5	6	7
Whole grade	20.7%	12.1%	11.1%	7.8%	7.5%	6.7%
Above-average	19.9%	11.1%	6.5%	5.6%	3.9%	1.7%
Below-average	21.3%	12.7%	17.5%	10.9%	11.1%	11.8%

Handwriting Rating (1-3)—Narration						
	Grade					
	2	3	4	5	6	7
Whole grade	1.3	1.9	2.0	2.0	2.1	2.3
Above-average	1.3	1.8	2.1	2.0	2.5	2.5
Below-average	1.3	2.0	1.8	2.0	1.8	2.0

Handwriting Rating (1-3)—Exposition						
	Grade					
	2	3	4	5	6	7
Whole grade	1.3	1.8	1.6	2.1	2.1	2.3
Above-average	1.5	1.8	1.9	2.1	2.5	2.5
Below-average	1.2	1.8	1.2	2.0	1.8	2.0

presented, we have corrected the grammar and mechanics in the content examples but have made no corrections in the examples for form. A copy of each sample, in the student's handwriting, accompanies the uncorrected version.

It can be seen in the table that, at grade 3, the students generally produced stories that were composed of lists of loosely connected sentences and ideas (rated at 2.3 out of 4). At grade 5, the stories were slightly more interesting and contained slightly more varied presentations of facts, with some explicit connections made between those facts (rated at 2.8—a half-point higher than at grade 3). At grade 7, the average paper again was slightly more interesting and connected than that produced at grade 5 (rated at 3.3—a half-point higher than at grade 5). Few students, however, even at grade 7, produced stories

Table 4-7 Content versus form, narration and exposition combined

	Grade					
	2	3	4	5	6	7
Content (whole grade)	1.7	2.2	2.4	2.9	2.6	3.1
Form (whole grade)	1.3	1.6	1.7	2.0	2.1	2.2

that were developed using strategies such as cause and effect, illustration, example, or detail; most stories were slightly sophisticated enumerations of facts.

Table 4-8 also illustrates the fact that the students had greater problems on form than they did on content in their narratives. At grade 3, the students exhibited severe sentence-structure problems—including fragments and run-on sentences—as well as grammatical and mechanical problems (rated at 1.9). At grade 5, the students still exhibited many of the same problems with form; their form rating was virtually the same as that of the grade 3 students (2.0). Even at grade 7, the students continued to have sentence-structure and other grammatical and mechanical problems (rated at 2.3). Students' average ratings never reached 3.0 (a few isolated errors) or 4.0 (only one or two errors) at any grade. Thus, on narration, although content improved steadily with successive grades, form remained problematic. In fact, the difference between the students' average form and content ratings grows with successive grades—from a half-point difference to a full-point difference.

On exposition, as on narration, content generally improved with successive grades; however, the students' form ratings at each grade were virtually the same. Table 4-9 presents examples of students' expository writing at grades 3, 5, and 7. These samples received both content and form ratings that approximated the mean for their grade. Again, in order to draw attention to the ideas being presented, we have corrected the grammar and mechanics in the content examples but have made no corrections in the examples for form. A copy of each sample, in the student's handwriting, accompanies the uncorrected version.

At each grade, there is about a three-quarter to a full-point difference between form and content ratings. In addition, while students' content ratings improve somewhat over grades, their form ratings do not. The students at grade 7 have about the same ratings on form as the students at grade 3, consistently exhibiting sentence-structure problems (such as run-on sentences) coupled with other grammatical and mechanical problems (with scores around 2.0).

The tendency that we found for this sample of low-income children to have better ideas than ways of expressing them successfully in their writing is confirmed in other research. For example, Shaughnessy (1977) found this same tendency among a sample of open-admissions (largely low-income) college students whom she termed "basic writers." She noted that these older, low-income students often are unfamiliar with "what might be called the dialect of formal writing . . . The result is . . . often a grotesque mixture of rudimentary errors, formal jargon, and strained syntax" (p. 45). Shaughnessy also noted that these students "know more about sentences than they can initially demonstrate as writers" (pp. 88–89). We found that the students' difficulty with form may well have a limiting effect on the overall maturity of their writing. This may be especially true for the below-average readers, who seemed to have particular problems in dealing with the multiple constraints of the writing task (see Flower and Hayes, 1980).

Vocabulary

The students as a group also had particular difficulty with the use of any but the most common words. Across grades, most of their production consisted of the shorter, more concrete words that are more characteristic of conversation or oral language than of print. We compared the children's production with the Dale list of 3,000 words known to 80 percent of fourth graders (see Table 4-5). On narration, only about 1 percent of the children's production was unfamiliar to the Dale list. On exposition, only about 3 percent of the words used were not on the Dale list; and more than half of these consisted of proper nouns (for instance, names of places or of people that the children admired). We also compared the children's production with the Spache list of 1,000 common words. No more than about 10 percent of words in the students' narratives and 8 percent in their expositions were not on the Spache list. The most frequently used word that did not appear on the Spache list was "tomato," a word that students had to use because of the nature of the stimulus. If "tomato" had not been counted as unfamiliar, the percentage of unfamiliar Spache

Table 4-8 Mean form and content ratings and examples at grades 3, 5, and 7: Narration

Grade	Mean content rating (1 low to 4 high)	Mean form rating (1 low to 4 high)	Examples of writing[a]
3	2.3	1.9	DRN2—Content (content rating = 2.3) There was a woman who had tomatoes. She was holding them in her hands. She was looking at the other tomatoes, and she was going to buy them to have in her salad at home with her children for supper and hamburgers and tomatoes. DRN2—Form (form rating = 2.0) There was a women how had tomatoes. she was holding them in her hands she was looking at the other tomatoes and she was going to buy them to have them in her salad at home with her children for supper and hamburgers with tomatoes.

There was a women how had tomatoes.
she was holding them inher hands she was
looking at the othe tom atoes
and she was going to buy them to
have them in her saladat home
with her childrem for supper and
hamburgers with tomatoes.

5	2.8	2.0	AJN2—Content (content rating = 2.7) This is an old lady looking for some big, red, juicy tomatoes. She is going to buy some tomatoes; so, when she gets home, she might make salad to eat for lunch. She also might be picking up some tomatoes for her son's wife or a friend. After maybe a week, she will go back and get some more juicy tomatoes to eat or maybe lettuce this time. She might not even get vegetables anymore. She might get some nice lean meat and have a cookout and have meat, Coke, hamburgers, hot dogs, and fruit punch. AJN2—Form (form rating = 2.0) This is an old lady looking for some big red juicy tomatoe's. she is going to bye some tomatoes. She when she get's home she might make salad to eat for lunch, she also might be Picking up some tomatoe's for here son's wife or a friend. After maybe a week after she will go back and get some more juicy tomatoes to eat or maybe lettuce this time. She might not even get vegativbles anymore She might get some nice lene meat. and have a cook out and have meat, coke, hamburgers, hotdogs and fruit Punch.

This is am old lady looking for Some
big red juicy tomatoe's. she is going to
bye Some tomatoes. She when she get's home
She might make Salad to eat for lunch, She
also might be Picking up some tomtoe's for
here son's wife or a freind: After maybe
a week after She will go back and get
Some more juicy tomatoes to eat or maybe
lettuce this time. She might not even
get vegativbles any more She might get
Some nice lene meat. and have a cook out
and have meat, coke, hamburgers, hotdogs and
fruit Punch.

Table 4-8 (continued)

Grade	Mean content rating (1 low to 4 high)	Mean form rating (1 low to 4 high)	Examples of writing[a]
7	3.3	2.3	HCN2—Content (content rating = 3.0) This lady in the picture looks like she is in a shopping store. She looks like she wants tomatoes, and somebody is talking to her. And she stops to look to see who it is. This lady also looks like she is going to open the package to see if anything is wrong with the tomatoes, but she wants to see if anybody's looking at her. This may seem very funny, but she also looks like she is going to steal those tomatoes; but she tries the playoff and looks back to see if anybody is going to see her take them. She also looks like she picked them up to get them, but it was the wrong thing. And at that time somebody said, "Hi;" and she stopped to say, "Hi" back. And she was going to put the tomatoes back. HCN2—Form (form rating = 2.0) This lady in the picture looks like she in a shopping store. She looks like she wants tomatoes, and somebody talking to her and she stops to look how it is. This lady also looks like she going to open the package to see if anything a wrong with the tomatoes, but she wants to see if anybodys looking at her. This may seem very funny but she also looks like she going to steal those tomatoes, but she try the play off and look back to see if anybody going to see her take them. She also looks like she picked them up to get them but it was the wrong thing, and at that time somebody said Hi and she stoped to say hi back, And she was going to put the tomatoes back.

This lady in the picture looks like she in a shopping store. She looks like she wants tomatoes, and somebody talking to her and she stops to look how it is.

This lady also looks like she going to open the package to see if anything a wrong with the tomatoes, but she wants to see if anybodys looking at her,

This may seem very funny, but she also locks like she going to steal these tomatoes, but she try the play off and lock back to see if any body going to see her take them.

She also looks like she picked them up to get them but it was the wrong thing, and at that time some body said Hi and she stoped to say hi back, And she was going to put The tomatoes back,

---

a. Grammar and mechanics have been corrected in the content examples to draw the reader's attention to the ideas being presented. No corrections have been made in presenting the same examples for form. The reproductions of the handwritten samples have been reduced to about 60 percent of full size.

Table 4-9 Mean form and content ratings and examples at grades 3, 5, and 7: Exposition

Grade	Mean content rating (1 low to 4 high)	Mean form rating (1 low to 4 high)	Examples of writing[a]
3	2.0	1.3	DTE2—Content (content rating = 2.0) I look up to my mother because, when my father passed away, Mother helped me a lot of times. Well, usually my mom yells at me; but she doesn't mean it. She's helped me through bad times. She cheers me in good times. That's why I admire her. We live nice and happy. The End. DTE2—Form (form rating = 1.3) I look up to my Mother because when my farther passed away Mother helped me alot of times. We youselly my mom yells at me but she doesn't mean it shes helped me through bad time she cheer me on good times thats why I admire her we live nice and happy. The End. I look up to my Mother because when my farther passed away Mother helpe'd me alot of times. We youselly my mom yells at me but she doesn't mean it shes help- ed me through bad time she cheer me on good times thats Why I admired her we live nice and happy. The End

5	3.0	1.9	DHE2—Content (content rating = 3.0) Jim Rice is left field, and he is a baseball player like me and like my dad. He is almost as good as Jim Rice, but you can't be good all the time. But sometimes we can be better than them. Even when we're not, we're just as well out as him. Jim Rice is a great hitter too and a greater catcher than me, but I can still play ball till I am old enough to quit the game! P.S. I still like Jim Rice. DHE2—Form (form rating = 2.0) Jim Rice is left field and he is a baseball player like me and like my Dad he is allmost as good as Jim Rice. But you can't be good all the time. But sometimes we can be beater than them. Even when were not were gust as well out as him. Jim Rice is a great hitter to and a great cather than me but I can still play ball till I am old enough to quit the game! P.S. I still like Jim Rice

Jim Rice.

Jim Rice is left field and he is a
baseball player like me and like my
Dad he is allmost as good as Jim Rice
But you can't be good all the time.
But sometimes we can be beater than
them. Even when were not were gust as
well out as him. Jim Rice is a great
hitter ~~to~~ and a great cather than
me but I can still play ball
till I am old enough to quit
the game!
P.S. I still like Jim Rice

Table 4-9 (continued)

Grade	Mean content rating (1 low to 4 high)	Mean form rating (1 low to 4 high)	Examples of writing[a]
7	2.8	2.1	PGE2—Content (content rating = 2.7) I look up to my mother because I think I should. First of all, she feeds me, pays for my things, and does a lot more for me. Usually I look up to her; but sometimes I look up to my sister, too. She does a lot for me but not the same kind of things like my mother does. She helps me with my problems and does me favors; but we fight a lot, too. My friends are the ones who do the same as me. That's what usually makes my friends. And I also look up to my friends because they have the same kinds of problems. I have a lot of people to look up to, and they help me a lot. PGE2—Form (form rating = 2.0) I look up to my mother, because I think I should, first of all she feeds me, pays for my things & does alot more for me. Usually I look up to her, but sometimes I look up to my sister too, she does alot for me but not the same kind of things like my mother does, she helps me with my problems & does me favors, but we fight alot too. My friends are the ones who do the same as me, that's what usually make my friends & I also look up to my friends because they have the same kind of problems. I have alot of people to look up to & they help me alot.

I look up to my mother, because I think I should, first of all she feeds me, pays for my things + does alot more for me. Usually I look up to her, but sometimes I look up to my sister too, she does alot for me but not the same kind of things like my mother does, she helps me with my problems + does me favors, but we fight alot too. My friends are the ones who do the same as me, thats what usualy make my friends + I also look up to my friends because they have the same kind of problems. I have alot of people to look up to + they help me alot.

---

a. Grammar and mechanics have been corrected in the content examples to draw the reader's attention to the ideas being presented. No corrections have been made in presenting the same examples for form. The reproductions of the handwritten samples have been reduced to about 60 percent of full size.

words used would have been even lower. The extent and use of unfamiliar words did not change much over the grades and was equally low for above-average and below-average readers.

This difficulty with words of lower frequency is similar to that found for the word meaning test for reading (see Chapter 3) and for vocabulary measures using the WISC (see Chapter 5).

Precision

The students also did not fare especially well, in an absolute sense, on the precision measures of handwriting and spelling (see Table 4-6). At grades 2 and 3, their handwriting was rated as inconsistent and irregular; at grades 4 through 7, it was rated only slightly better. Few students, even at grades 6 and 7, were rated as having neat, stylized handwriting.

The students' spelling showed a similar trend. The percentage of misspelled words decreased dramatically from grade 2 (when students misspelled about 20 percent of the words in their narratives and expositions) to grade 3 (when students misspelled about 7 percent of their narrations and about 12 percent of their expositions). However, the percentage of misspellings did not then decrease much from grade to grade, a surprising fact given that the vocabulary they used was generally familiar—the kind of vocabulary the children would use in their everyday oral language. (See Chapter 3 for similar trends for spelling on the reading battery.)

Syntax and Organization

The syntax of the students' writing developed consistently. On both narration and exposition, the T-unit production of the older students (grades 4 to 7) was greater than that of the younger students (grades 2 and 3). The same trend was found for students' utterance length. The T-unit lengths of our population were equally long or longer than those produced by primarily middle-class children in other studies (for example, Hunt, 1965; O'Donnell, Griffin, and Norris, 1967; Heil, 1976; Loban, 1976). In fact, a closer examination reveals that their T-units were more similar in length to those that students of the same age from other studies used in their oral language (see O'Donnell, Griffin, and Norris, 1967; Loban, 1976; Jacobs, 1986).

Over grades, the organization of our students' writing was not strong. On narration, the youngest students (grades 2 and 3) relied on the simplest, list-like, temporal relation (for example, "and then") to describe the action in their stories. Older students (grades 4 to 7) wrote only slightly more complex stories, incorporating some cause and effect and conditional relations. On exposition, students across grades relied only on the simplest, list-like, additive relation (such as "and") to describe their reasons for admiring someone. They seemed to lack understanding of the structure of argument. Their organizational plan in exposition resembled that which they used in narration; in fact, they seemed to misapply the low-level "what next" strategy they had used in their narrations to their expositions (see Bereiter and Scardamalia, 1982). The organization the students used most often in narration and exposition—additive and temporal relations—is not sophisticated in an absolute sense; these relations are those used earliest in oral language and most frequently in writing (see Jacobs, 1986).

Summary

Most measures of the children's writing exhibited the same decelerative trend observed for reading: students' scores in grades 4 and 5 were higher than those of students in grades 2 and 3, but students' scores in grades 6 and 7 resembled those for students in grades 4 and 5. The below-average readers almost always scored lower on writing measures than the above-average readers.

None of the students' writing was "mature," in an absolute sense, at any grade. Even at grade 7 the children's writing was quite simple, with the kind of linguistic complexity and vocabulary typical of conversational, oral language—the kind of language children use before they enter school.

The students seemed to have creative ideas (that is, content) in their writing, but they had difficulty expressing those ideas in precise form and with precise vocabulary. These findings recall the strengths and difficulties the students had on the various reading tests. They had greater difficulty in defining, recognizing, and spelling words presented in isolation and in defining less common words at fourth grade and higher. At the same time, they scored better on tests of connected reading—reading comprehension and oral reading. Thus, on both the reading tests and the writing samples, the students did less well on tasks that required precision (for example, defining words, word recognition, and spelling).

The students generally fared better on narration—a genre with which they were familiar before entering school—than on exposition. At all grades, students relied on the structures they knew best (such as "and" or "and then"), on familiar vocabulary (for example, those words used at a conversational level), and on familiar background knowledge. The texts the students produced across grades, in fact, were very similar to reading materials that use language, structures, and ideas already familiar to students (for example, Stage 2 in Chall, 1983b; see Table 1-1).

Implications

Given the strong side of the children's writing—that they had creative ideas to express, especially on narration—and its weak side—that they lacked precise form and vocabulary with which to express their ideas, especially on exposition—what do we recommend to help the students, especially the below-average readers, to improve their writing?

In our classroom observations we found that the children were receiving little practice in producing extended pieces of writing. It was clear that the children needed more writing practice; the question was, what kind of writing? What little writing the children did produce in their classrooms was narrative or personal writing. It was characteristic of what has become popularly known as "process writing" (see Graves, 1983; Calkins, 1986), a kind of writing that encourages students to establish and maintain their own voices in their writing and allows them practice in fluency. Process writing can provide powerful strategies for students to think about what they are doing as they are writing (see Applebee, Langer, and Mullis, 1987, p. 37). It has been described as learning "by doing it and sharing it with real audiences, not by studying and applying abstract rhetorical principles in exercises which the teacher alone will read and judge" (Parker, 1979, quoted in Hillocks, 1986, p. 36). In the process writing approach, the teacher's chief task is to react and respond to the children's production with questions that, it is hoped, will lead the students to realize for themselves how they need to proceed in tackling a particular writing task (Hillocks, 1986, p. 119).

Is the process writing approach useful for these children? There is evidence that the freedom given to children in this approach may be enriching for some, but it may not be optimal for our students given their strengths and weaknesses. Hillocks (1986) found from a meta-analysis of the research on writing instruction that the "natural process" (process writing) of writing instruction does not produce the best results. Among its weaknesses is that, although it tells students what is strong or weak in their writing, it may not supply students with criteria for how to identify problems and strengths in their writing or how to correct or avoid particular problems (Hillocks, 1986, p. 224). Indeed, this is just what our population seemed to need.

The National Assessment of Educational Progress (Applebee, Langer, and Mullis, 1987) reports that focus on process writing has probably led to more time spent on writing in classrooms; however, the recent NAEP report on writing did not find proportionate improvement in writing given the increased time (p. 34). The report calls for additional kinds of instruction that will teach students—directly—how to use their reflection about their writing in meaningful reading and writing-task situations (p. 37): "Simply providing students with exposure to new activities may not be enough to ensure they learn how to use these skills effectively for improving their reading, writing, and reasoning. Students may need to have more direct instruction about when and how to use such approaches, to have more practice in using them to solve problems in their own reading and writing, and to be evaluated in a manner that allows them to use the skills they develop" (pp. 38–39). This recommendation is similar to that of Hillocks (1986), who advocated that students be shown *how* as well as *what* to learn—that they be provided with highly structured problem-solving activities in peer groups that encourage inquiry and analysis of content.

For the children in our sample, who already seem fairly confident and fluent in their writing—especially in narrative and personal writing—there is an additional need for the more structured approach recommended by Hillocks and Applebee. Our population needs not only encouragement to write, but also understanding of what rhetorical conventions to use and how to use them appropriately given the nature of the particular genre they are using. Those children who do not arrive at school with such knowledge depend upon direct instruction in writing not just to help them to establish and maintain their own voice but also to acquire the ability to employ conventional forms (see Cazden, 1987, cited in Delpit, 1988). Delpit calls for a writing curriculum that both provides opportunity for those who already know content or skills to exhibit that knowledge and also teaches new information to those who may not have already acquired that knowledge (1988, p. 19). Ideally, skills practice should be couched in meaningful instructional contexts that illustrate application rather than in isolated exercises.

Thus, the best curriculum for these children does not appear to be a process *versus* skills approach, but rather a judicious combination of the two. They require continued opportunity to develop their fluency but also need direct, structured instruction in organization and form and in genres and syntax with which they are less familiar. For syntactic instruction to be meaningful, students should have an opportunity to experiment with producing their own structures—drawing upon but also expanding upon the options they already have at their command in their oral language.

The students in our study could also profit from earlier, increased, and more direct vocabulary instruction—especially of vocabulary that is less common in everyday spoken language and more characteristic of academic discourse. Even the writing samples of the best readers used only the most concrete, most commonly used, highly frequent words. The content of their writing, ultimately, was probably affected by the limited vocabulary with which they expressed themselves. The classroom observations indicated that, overall, the children received little instruction in vocabulary.

The students read and wrote mostly narration. The books children chose to read on their own were usually popular novels—narrations rather than more literary or expository texts (Chall, Snow, et al., 1982, pp. 4–44). Since students draw upon their outside reading for ideas in their writing (Juel, 1988), it is important that they read more than narratives, including more expository prose.

The children could easily be asked to produce expository writing in the context of content instruction. When integrated with content instruction, writing can become a meaningful exercise in application rather than an exercise in form only; it becomes a vehicle for learning a more academic vocabulary as well as form that is more characteristic of academic language (see Hillocks, 1986). Such writing exercises can include observation notebooks (common in a science curriculum), dialectic journals (also commonly called dialogue journals or double-entry notebooks; see Berthoff, 1984), or other writing that allows students the chance to integrate their background knowledge with new information (see Stotsky, 1984).

Thus, the kind of writing practice that the children in our sample require exceeds exercise in fluency and voice. These children need instruction in how to apply particular skills in the process of constructing meaning in their writing. They must also be challenged to use structures and vocabulary less common to oral language and narration—beyond what they already know.

Especially in the early grades, the students in our sample showed that they had the ability to generate ideas and use language creatively. The content of their essays was generally good. But their writing instruction, instead of going beyond the children's experiences with language, seems to have been circular in nature—simply providing more practice with what they already knew. These children needed guidance in exploring the concepts and structures of the world of written discourse.

5

Language Development

We studied the children's language as well as their reading and writing, since literacy is intimately related to language development. There are different viewpoints on the importance of the role played by language in the acquisition of literacy. Some tend to put a greater or lesser emphasis on language development as a factor in reading and writing achievement; others say that the importance of language for literacy varies with the stage of development—that it is less important in the primary grades and more important in the intermediate grades and later.

Our major questions with regard to language and literacy were: How does the language of low-income children develop during grades 2 through 7? Is the course of language development similar to or different from that of their reading and writing? How does their language relate to their reading and writing development?

Three measures of language—vocabulary, grammar, and metalinguistic (language) awareness—developed for the study by Carol Chomsky, were administered individually at the same time as the reading and writing measures—to all 30 students at the end of grades 2, 4, and 6 and again a year later when the students were completing grades 3, 5, and 7.

Vocabulary

Two vocabulary tests were given, both based on the vocabulary subtest of the Wechsler Intelligence Scale for Children (Revised) (WISC-R).

Vocabulary Knowledge. The students were asked to define words on the WISC-R vocabulary test. Credit was given for words students knew or those with which they were familiar. A word was considered "known" even if the student's explanation of the word was incomplete or reflected only partial knowledge. For example, for the word *gamble,* acceptable answers were "want some beer and can gamble to get it," or "shouldn't do—get money." For *diamond,* an acceptable response was "ring or necklace or pearl." Thus, the criteria used for the vocabulary knowledge score gave us a broad view of the number of words with which the children were familiar; analysis of accuracy and depth of description was reserved for the other vocabulary measure.

Precision and Sophistication of Word Definitions. This measure gave the children credit for use of sophisticated language in a response, for the maturity of their responses, and for reports of two meanings in the case of ambiguous words. Credit was given for the use of sophisticated vocabulary and phraseology (for example, *diamond:* "a valuable rock, a precious stone"; *donkey:* "an animal related to the horse family"). Credit was also given for precise and advanced vocabulary used in definitions. Another aspect of sophistication and precision was beginning a definition with the same part of speech as the word being defined (for instance, defining *nail* as "sharp metal object," "holds things together," "something that goes into wood," or "piece of metal" rather than "fix stuff" or "sticks to your finger"). Finally, credit was given when a student provided both meanings for an ambiguous word (such as *nail*) while others gave only one.

From the total WISC-R word list, six items were selected for this test: *nail, alphabet, donkey, thief, brave,* and *diamond.* Since all the children in the study responded to these six words, the precision/sophistication features were well represented.

Results of Vocabulary Assessments

Table 5-1 presents the mean scores for vocabulary knowledge in the first and second years of the study for the entire group and shows the gains the children made over one year. The table also notes the differences in the children's scores from grades 2 to 4 and 4 to 6, and from grades 3 to 5 and 5 to 7.

The table shows that vocabulary knowledge, based on "lenient" scoring of definitions of the words on the WISC-R, increased at a faster pace in the earlier than in the later grades. This is reflected in gains by grade and in the gains in the second year as compared to the first year. When we view the course of development from grades 2 to 7, we find that it is similar to that for reading and writing—stronger development from grades 2 to 3, and deceleration from grades 4 to 7.

Table 5-1 Vocabulary knowledge by grades

Mean scores by grades				
First year	Second year		First to second year gains	Percentage of gain in terms of year 1
Grade 2 57.50	Grade 3 68.87		11.37	20%
Grade 4 76.66	Grade 5 87.08		10.42	14%
Grade 6 80.00	Grade 7 86.25		6.25	8%
Differences from grade 2 to 4	+19.16		Differences from grade 3 to 5	+18.21
Differences from grade 4 to 6	+3.34		Differences from grade 5 to 7	−0.83

Table 5-2 presents the scores for both the above-average and below-average readers. The above- and below-average readers seemed to differ most in the second and third grades. By the fourth grade, and through the seventh grade, however, the scores of the above-average and below-average readers were quite similar. This trend is different from that for the reading and writing measures, where we found that differences between the above-average and below-average readers increased with succeeding grades.

Table 5-3 presents the results for precision and sophistication of word definitions for each of the grades for the first and second years, together with gains per year. This measure shows a strong decelerative trend for the whole group after grade 3. The gains are considerable from grade 2 to 3, but they are minimal from grade 4 on and are particularly low from grade 6 to 7.

When we compared the more lenient measure of vocabulary knowledge with the more stringent measure of vocabulary precision and sophistication, we found similar trends: both decelerate around the fourth grade. If there is a difference between the two measures, it is the greater gains on the precision and sophistication measure, particularly from grade 2 to grade 3. Generally, for all the grades, there is a greater, more consistent increase in scores by grade on the precision and sophistication measure than on vocabulary familiarity.

Table 5-4 presents the results on the precision and sophistication measure by above-average and below-average readers. The trends are quite similar to those found for vocabulary knowledge (see Table 5-2);

we found greater gains for both groups between grades 2 and 3 and decreasing gains after grade 4. The above-average and the below-average readers tended to differ more after grade 4 than they did on the vocabulary knowledge measure.

Overall, the developmental trends for the precision and sophistication vocabulary measures and vocabulary knowledge are similar to the trends found for the word meaning test that was part of the reading test battery (see Chapter 3). On all vocabulary measures, the fourth-grade slump was evident; the students' scores increased relatively little after grade 3.

Grammar

The grammar test measured syntactic knowledge based on four separate syntactic subtests. These measures assessed the children's knowledge of constructions that require relatively sophisticated syn-

Table 5-2 Trends in vocabulary knowledge by above-average and below-average readers

	Mean scores by grades		First to second year gains	Percentage of gain in terms of year 1
	Grade 2	Grade 3		
Above-average readers	48.75	63.75	15.00	31%
Difference from total group	(−8.75)	(−5.12)		
Below-average readers	63.33	70.83	7.50	12%
Difference from total group	(+5.83)	(+1.96)		
	Grade 4	Grade 5		
Above-average readers	77.85	89.28	11.43	15%
Difference from total group	(+1.19)	(+2.20)		
Below-average readers	75.00	84.00	9.00	12%
Difference from total group	(−1.66)	(−3.08)		
	Grade 6	Grade 7		
Above-average readers	81.25	87.50	6.25	8%
Difference from total group	(+1.25)	(+1.25)		
Below-average readers	78.75	85.00	6.25	8%
Difference from total group	(−1.25)	(−1.25)		

Table 5-3 Precision and sophistication of word definitions

Mean scores by grades		First to second year gains	Percentage of gain in terms of year 1
First year	Second year		
Grade 2 9.50	Grade 3 25.00	15.50	163%
Grade 4 25.00	Grade 5 33.75	8.75	35%
Grade 6 30.63	Grade 7 36.25	5.62	18%
Differences from grade 2 to 4	+15.50	Differences from grade 3 to 5	+8.75
Differences from grade 4 to 6	+5.63	Differences from grade 5 to 7	+2.50

tactic knowledge that goes beyond the basic grammatical constructions acquired during the early childhood years.

Four kinds of measures were used to assess each child in the study:

1. *Ask* + wh- clause. The first test assessed the children's knowledge of a complex construction involving the verb *ask,* namely the subject assignment to an infinitive verb in a wh-complement clause following *ask.* For example, in the following two constructions the subject of the verb *eat* is different: 1. John *told* Mary what to eat. (John told Mary what *she* should eat.) 2. John *asked* Mary what to eat. (John asked Mary what *he* should eat.) In the first example the subject of *eat* is Mary, but in the second case the subject of *eat* is John. The first example follows the normal pattern of English; the second is an exceptional pattern, which is subject to late acquisition by many children. Children who have not mastered the exceptional property of the verb *ask* assign an incorrect subject to the complement verb and often fail to understand that a question is being asked.

2. *Promise* + complement clause. The next test assessed the children's ability to assign the correct subject to an infinitive verb following *promise,* as in: 1. John *told* Mary to shovel the driveway. 2. John *promised* Mary to shovel the driveway. Again, the first example is a normal pattern and the second is an exceptional construction. Children who do not understand the exceptional properties of the verb *promise* assign an incorrect subject to the infinitive complement verb in this construction.

3. *Although.* Another test was designed to assess children's knowl-

edge of a particular complex construction following *although*. Note the different referent of the phrase *done the same* in the following sentences: 1. Mother scolded Gloria for eating the banana, and I would have *done the same.* 2. Mother scolded Gloria for eating the banana, although I would have *done the same.* In the first example, I would have scolded Gloria, but in the second, I would have eaten the banana. Children who do not yet command this complex construction have difficulty in assigning the correct referent, especially in the second sentence.

This test also included a check on the children's knowledge of the meaning of the word *although* and their ability to use it in a simpler sentence-completion task (for example, Although it was raining outside, I ____).

As it turned out, none of the children in the study succeeded in the complex task using *done the same* in either the first or the second year, so it provided no basis for comparisons. However, the sentence com-

Table 5-4 Precision and sophistication of word definitions by above-average and below-average readers

	Mean scores by grades		First to second year gains	Percentage of gain in terms of year 1
	Grade 2	Grade 3		
Above-average readers	11.25	25.00	13.75	122%
Difference from total group	(+1.75)	0.0		
Below-average readers	8.33	25.00	16.67	200%
Difference from total group	(−1.17)	0.0		
	Grade 4	Grade 5		
Above-average readers	27.85	39.28	11.43	41%
Difference from total group	(+2.85)	(+5.53)		
Below-average readers	21.00	26.00	5.00	24%
Difference from total group	(−4.00)	(−7.75)		
	Grade 6	Grade 7		
Above-average readers	36.25	45.00	8.75	24%
Difference from total group	(+5.62)	(+8.75)		
Below-average readers	25.00	27.50	2.50	10%
Difference from total group	(−5.63)	(−8.75)		

pletion task did prove to be a useful discriminator; therefore, the simpler measure was used in our total grammar score.

4. Tag questions. The final grammar measure assessed children's ability to construct tag questions to turn a statement into a question, as in: John likes to go to the movies, doesn't he? Children were told the first part of the sentence and asked to add the correct tag. This task requires subject and verb identification, insertion of a pronoun, and use of an auxiliary verb—all relatively intricate syntactic abilities that tend to be acquired late by children.

Results of Grammar Assessments

Table 5-5 presents the combined results on the four grammar tests. The table shows greater gains in the earlier grades and lesser gains from grade 4 on. As with the vocabulary tests, increases in grammar slowed from grade 4 on; the students experienced smaller, more limited gains from grade 4 on than from grade 2 to 3.

The differences between scores of the above-average and below-average readers tended to be inconsistent over grades (Table 5-6). In several instances, the below-average readers scored higher on the grammar composite than did the above-average readers; and overall differences between the two groups were often relatively small.

Language Awareness

The language awareness test (or test of metalinguistic awareness) measured students' abilities to view language objectively and to for-

Table 5-5 Grammar composite

Mean scores by grades			
First year	Second year	First to second year gains	Percentage of gain in terms of year 1
Grade 2 57.25	Grade 3 85.00	27.75	48%
Grade 4 68.20	Grade 5 82.29	14.09	20%
Grade 6 71.50	Grade 7 83.42	13.42	18%
Differences from grade 2 to 4	+10.95	Differences from grade 3 to 5	−2.71
Differences from grade 4 to 6	+3.30	Differences from grade 5 to 7	+1.13

Table 5-6 Grammar composite by above-average and below-average readers

	Mean scores by grades		First to second year gains	Percentage of gain in terms of year 1
	Grade 2	Grade 3		
Above-average	66.25	76.25	10.00	15%
Below-average	51.25	90.83	39.58	77%
Difference	+15.00	−14.58		
	Grade 4	Grade 5		
Above-average	73.57	85.21	11.64	15%
Below-average	60.70	78.20	17.50	28%
Difference	+12.87	+7.01		
	Grade 6	Grade 7		
Above-average	68.25	82.37	14.12	21%
Below-average	74.75	86.16	11.41	15%
Difference	−6.50	−3.79		

mulate judgments about its properties. Metalinguistic ability has proved to be a good indicator of linguistic maturity and ability to manipulate language effectively (Davis, 1968; Carroll, 1971). A composite language awareness score was constructed from a set of separate metalinguistic subtests.

1. *Sentence Acceptability* (grammaticality). This test elicited judgments from children about the acceptability of sentences of four different types:

a. Fully grammatical and plausible. (There were four people at the school.)

b. Fully grammatical but implausible. (The pencil weighed five pounds.)

c. Systematically anomalous. (The rock is very angry.)

d. Syntactically deviant. (The men looked at herself in the mirror.)

Success on this test required rejecting sentences of type d, recognizing the structural acceptability of type c, and accepting types a and b.

2. *Illicit Comparison.* This task assessed children's ability to explain the deviance of sentences that make illegitimate comparisons, such as: This math problem is harder than that rock. To succeed on this problem, children were required to recognize the differences in the use of the word *hard,* in one case meaning difficult and in the other meaning hard to the touch. Focusing on the ambiguities between

abstract and concrete properties is a fairly sophisticated ability that children tend to acquire late.

3. *Illicit Conjunction.* This test assessed the children's ability to explain the deviance of sentences that combine other similar sentences in a way that is unacceptable. In this example, we can say either of the first two sentences independently, but we cannot combine them as in the third sentence: 1. John caught the measles. 2. John caught the fast ball. 3. John caught the measles and the fast ball. Recognizing and explaining the different uses of a word like *catch* in such a sentence are also abilities that children typically acquire late.

4. *Jokes and Riddles.* The final language awareness test assessed the children's ability to explain what is funny about jokes and riddles that rely on ambiguity for their humor. For example: Where would you go to see a man eating fish? To a seafood restaurant. In the question it seems that the fish is eating the man, but the answer turns the table so that the man is eating the fish. The children were asked to explain what was funny about jokes like this, and similar jokes that contained lexical ambiguities, surface-structure ambiguities, or deep-structure ambiguities.

Table 5-7 presents the results of the language awareness composite based on these four separate metalinguistic tests. The greatest percentage of gain occurred from grade 2 to 3, but the greatest gains in actual scores occurred later—from grade 4 to 5. As with the other tests, this was followed by a deceleration, this time from grade 6 to 7. The results for the above-average and below-average groups were less consistent, however (Table 5-8). The above-average group did not outscore the below-average group until grade 4, but beginning with grade 5 they were considerably ahead of the below-average group.

Total Language Score

The students' scores on the separate language tests were combined into a single Total Language Score; each component received the following weights:

Vocabulary knowledge	40%
Vocabulary precision and sophistication	10%
Grammar composite	30%
Language awareness composite	20%

The patterns of development from grade 2 through grade 7 for total language (Table 5-9) are similar to the developmental trends found for

Table 5-7 Language awareness by grades

Mean scores by grades		First to second year gains	Percentage of gain in terms of year 1
First year	Second year		
Grade 2 16.66	Grade 3 29.99	13.33	80%
Grade 4 40.75	Grade 5 62.28	21.53	53%
Grade 6 40.72	Grade 7 58.68	17.96	44%
Differences from grade 2 to 4	+24.09	Differences from grade 3 to 5	+32.29
Differences from grade 4 to 6	−0.03	Differences from grade 5 to 7	−3.60

Table 5-8 Trends in language awareness by above-average and below-average readers

	Mean scores by grades		First to second year gains	Percentage of gain in terms of year 1
	Grade 2	Grade 3		
Above-average	16.66	24.99	8.33	50%
Difference from total group	(0.0)	(−5.00)		
Below-average	16.66	33.33	16.67	100%
Difference from total group	(0.0)	(+3.34)		
	Grade 4	Grade 5		
Above-average	47.37	72.72	25.35	54%
Difference from total group	(+6.62)	(+10.44)		
Below-average	31.49	47.66	16.17	51%
Difference from total group	(−9.26)	(−14.62)		
	Grade 6	Grade 7		
Above-average	46.45	61.65	15.20	33%
Difference from total group	(+5.73)	(+2.97)		
Below-average	34.99	54.71	19.72	56%
Difference from total group	(−5.73)	(−3.97)		

Table 5-9 Total language score

Mean scores by grades		First to second year gains	Percentage of gain in terms of year 1
First year	Second year		
Grade 2 44.45	Grade 3 61.09	16.64	37%
Grade 4 61.78	Grade 5 75.31	13.53	22%
Grade 6 64.65	Grade 7 75.33	10.68	17%
Differences from grade 2 to 4	+17.33	Differences from grade 3 to 5	+14.22
Differences from grade 4 to 6	+2.87	Differences from grade 5 to 7	+0.02

writing and reading: the students made the strongest gains from grade 2 to grade 3, and deceleration set in at about fourth or fifth grade.

The above-average and below-average readers show similar trends in development on the total language measure: the greatest gains for both groups were from grade 2 to grade 3; both experienced smaller gains beginning at grade 4, and both groups continued to decelerate from grade 4 through grade 7 (Table 5-10).

What is of interest in these composite language scores is the relatively small differences found between the above-average and below-average readers. Not only are the differences small, but on some of the measures, and for some grades, the below-average readers had higher scores than the above-average readers.

Summary of Language Measures

The various language measures used for the study—vocabulary, grammar, and language awareness—revealed similar developmental patterns: larger gains in the earlier grades and decelerating gains in the later grades. On the whole, the trends are similar to those found for the various measures of reading (Chapter 3) and writing (Chapter 4). However, the language scores tend to be less consistent. Also of interest are the smaller differences found on most of the language measures (except for vocabulary), as compared to the reading and

Table 5-10 Total language score for above-average and below-average readers

	Mean scores by grades		First to second year gains	Percentage of gain in terms of year 1
	Grade 2	Grade 3		
Above-average	43.83	55.62	11.79	27%
Below-average	44.87	64.74	19.87	44%
Differences	−1.04	−9.12		
	Grade 4	Grade 5		
Above-average	65.47	79.69	14.22	22%
Below-average	56.60	69.19	12.59	22%
Differences	−8.87	−10.50		
	Grade 6	Grade 7		
Above-average	65.89	76.24	10.35	16%
Below-average	63.42	74.12	10.70	17%
Differences	−2.47	−2.12		

writing measures, between the above-average and below-average readers.

The implication that may be drawn from these findings is that the grammar and language awareness measures are related differently to reading than are the vocabulary and the writing measures. This can be seen from the small differences in scores among the above-average and below-average readers on the grammar and metalinguistic tests. Indeed, we found that on these measures the below-average readers occasionally scored higher than the above-average readers.

Thus it would seem that the influence of language on reading varies by level of development and by the language component—whether vocabulary, syntax, or language awareness. In the following chapter we make further comparisons of reading, writing, and language development.

6

Interrelations among Reading, Writing, and Language

There has been a long-standing consensus among researchers and teachers that all aspects of language learning are highly interrelated. John B. Carroll's analysis of the development of reading comprehension (1977) and the longitudinal studies of Walter Loban (1963, 1976) present strong theoretical and empirical evidence that reading development is, to a great extent, dependent on students' language and cognitive development as well as on their development of reading skills. These researchers and others have also shown that the relationships among language, cognition, and reading become stronger as students move from the earlier to the higher levels of reading development (Singer, 1962; Chall, 1967, 1983a, 1983b; Holmes, 1976; Stanovich, 1986). To shed further light on the relationship of reading, writing, and language for the low-income children in our sample, we undertook two cross-domain factor analyses and a comparison of the developmental trends for their reading, writing, and language.

Factor Analyses

Two separate factor analyses were performed—one for the pretest data (grades 2, 4, and 6) and one for the posttest data (grades 3, 5, and 7). Included in both the pretest and posttest factor analyses were all six subtests from the reading battery (word recognition, phonics, oral reading, spelling, word meaning, and silent reading comprehension), selected measures from the narrative writing sample (holistic score, number of words produced in 10 minutes, words not on the Spache list of 1,000, and ratings of organization, form, and content), and all of the language measures (vocabulary knowledge, precision and sophistication of word definitions, grammar, and language awareness).* The factor analyses were run on the scores for the 30 students who completed both the pretests and the posttests.

We undertook the factor analyses to gain additional insights into what was influencing what. Was language strongly related to reading, and, if so, to what reading components and at what grades? Did some language measures have a lesser impact on reading and writing than others, and, if so, on which components of reading and writing? A factor analysis can help answer such questions by indicating common factors running through the various tests and the potency of these factors. Factor loadings indicate the strengths that the various tests have on a given factor.

Results

We present first the results of the factor analysis on the scores for the first year, when the children were in grades 2, 4, and 6 (Table 6-1). The table shows that four factors emerged. Our name for each factor was based on an analysis of the features common to the tests that showed high loadings on that particular factor. The higher the coefficients noted for the different measures, the more important they are in contributing to the factor. In order of their strength, we labeled the following factors: (1) literacy: reading and writing, (2) language and writing, (3) language, and (4) writing and word meanings.

The strongest factor was "literacy: reading and writing"; its highest loadings were from various reading tests: oral reading (.85), phonics (.83), word recognition (.82), and silent reading comprehension (.77). Moderate loadings were found for two of the writing measures: ratings for the content (.61) and form (.53) of the students' samples.

Factor 1 is of special interest because it contains four of the six tests from the reading battery; only spelling and word meanings from the reading battery are not included in this factor. The most potent inputs are from the three measures of reading that require accurate word recognition—oral reading, phonics, and word recognition. Silent reading is also strong on Factor 1 but not as strong as measures of accuracy of word recognition and decoding.

Factor 2, which we named "language and writing," had loadings

*The writing measures used in the factor analyses were selected because they represented a variety of interrelated aspects of writing, and preliminary analyses showed they were strongly correlated with overall, holistic scores.

Table 6-1 Factors for the first year, total sample

Factor 1 Literacy: Reading and Writing		Factor 2 Language and Writing		Factor 3 Language		Factor 4 Writing and Word Meanings	
Word recognition	.82	Word meaning	.57	Word meaning	.51	Number of words outside of Spache	.45
Oral reading	.85	Writing: number of words (production)	.63	Grammar	.74	Writing: content	.44
Silent reading	.77	Number of words outside of Spache	.55	Total language	.73	Writing: form	.49
Phonics	.83	Language awareness	.81			Precision and sophisticated words	.48
Writing: content	.61						
Writing: form	.53						

mainly from the language measures—language awareness (.81) and word meaning (.57)—and from the writing measures—production (.63) and words outside of the Spache 1,000 list of common words (.55). Factor 2 points to the strong relationship between writing and facility with language. This factor suggests that the children who were stronger on the writing measures of production (number of words written) and number of less common words were also stronger in language awareness and word meaning.

Factor 3, which we named the "language factor," had loadings mainly from the language tests (grammar, total language, and word meaning). Factor 4, "writing and word meanings," had sizable loadings from the writing measures (words outside of the Spache 1,000 common words and ratings of content and form) and also from vocabulary (precision and sophistication of word definitions). This factor suggests that those children who were better writers had greater facility with using less familiar vocabulary.

In sum, the factor analysis based on the children's scores in grades 2, 4, and 6 indicates that the strongest factor for all of the reading, writing, and language measures is a literacy (reading/writing) factor, with the strongest loadings from accuracy in word recognition and decoding. The other three factors, concerned mainly with language and writing, have strong loadings from word meanings and vocabulary. Language awareness also loads relatively strongly on the writing and language factors. The weakest influence of all the language measures seems to be that of grammar.

The second factor analysis on the posttest scores (grades 3, 5, and 7) produced generally similar results, but there were some differences (Table 6-2). The strongest factor was labeled the "reading factor." The three components that loaded highest on this factor were silent reading comprehension (.81) and two measures of meaning vocabulary—the vocabulary knowledge score from the WISC-R (.82) and the word meaning test from the reading test battery (.78). All of these components were measures of the meaning aspects of reading. The two other loadings on the reading factor were phonics (.68) and spelling (.52), factors more closely related to word recognition and to the decoding aspects of reading. Thus, in the second factor analysis, when the students were a year older, the first factor is still a reading factor, but the highest loadings are for meaning-related aspects of reading. The first factor analysis found the word recognition and decoding aspects to be stronger.

We labeled Factor 2 "literacy: precision" since it contained high

Table 6-2 Factors for the posttests, total sample

Factor 1 Reading		Factor 2 Literacy: Precision		Factor 3 Writing		Factor 4 Language		Factor 5 Language	
Word meaning	.78	Word recognition	.68	Number of words in sample	.57	Language awareness	.95	Grammar	.90
Silent reading comprehension	.81	Oral reading	.81	Holistic score	.58	Total language	.65	Total language	.47
Spelling	.52	Spelling	.73	Writing organization	.84	Subscore grammar	.78		
Phonics	.68	Vocabulary knowledge	.54	Writing: content	.85				
Vocabulary knowledge	.82	Writing: form	.81						
		Word precision and sophistication	.62						

loadings from assessments of reading, writing, and language that contained aspects of accuracy and precision. In particular, form in writing (.81) and oral reading (.81) both had the highest loadings, followed by spelling (.73). We named Factor 3 "writing" because all of its loadings were obtained from the writing measures, and Factors 4 and 5 were named "language" since they contained loadings only from the language tasks.

Discussion of Findings

Both factor analyses indicated the central role played by reading, which emerged as a stronger factor than either the writing or the language measures. Writing seems to have been the next most potent measure. Finally, the language measures, although lowest in potency, were also strongly related to both reading and writing. At least two aspects of reading and writing seemed to come through on both of the factor analyses. For reading they were the distinctions between the well-known dimensions of word recognition and decoding versus word meaning and comprehension; for writing they were the distinctions between form and content. The factor analyses showed that it is possible to be strong on either one of the dimensions but weak on the others.

Although reading was the strongest factor on both factor analyses, the loadings for the reading factors were somewhat different on the pretests and the posttests. The results of our factor analyses seem to reflect the changes that took place in one year between the two tests. During the first year, when the group as a whole ranged from second to sixth grade (with a median of grade 4), their reading achievement had stronger associations with decoding and word recognition. When they were in grades 3, 5, and 7 (with a median of grade 5), their reading achievement was more strongly related to the meaning aspects of reading. These findings are supported by the other findings from the study and by the research literature on the development of language and literacy (Singer, 1962; Chall, 1967, 1983a; Holmes, 1976; Loban, 1976) as well as by developmental theories of reading (Chall, 1969, 1979, 1983b, 1989; Carroll, 1977). These studies propose that, for all children, achievement in beginning reading is more highly associated with word recognition and decoding than with language and cognition. Beyond the primary grades, however, reading achievement is increasingly associated with the development of language and cognition. Indeed, by the middle grades, children's knowledge of word meanings has the highest correlation with reading comprehension (Davis, 1968, 1972; R. L. Thorndike, 1973–74; Anderson and Freebody, 1981; Chall and Stahl, 1985). Our analyses indicated that, as the reading tasks become more advanced and sophisticated, word meanings become more important than word recognition and decoding (see Chapter 3).

On both factor analyses, reading seems to be related more to writing than to language. When reading is related to language, it is related more to the vocabulary measures than to language awareness or to grammar. Does this mean that language awareness and grammar are relatively unimportant in explaining the reading achievement of our population? It is hard to say. One reason for the relatively low association may stem from the fact that the grammar and language awareness measures developed for and used in this study tended to have ceiling effects at about grade 3. The relative easiness of the language tests may have reduced the possibility of finding stronger relationships with reading. On the other hand, vocabulary scores continued to increase with age and maturity. Thus, the association of vocabulary with reading comprehension and other reading scores continued through grade 7.

Another possibility is that grammar and language awareness tests are less important for reading development than they are for writing development. Generally, the grammar and language awareness scores had higher correlations with the writing than with the reading scores. Indeed, it seems logical that writing, long considered the more expressive aspect of literacy, would require more awareness and precise knowledge of language structures than reading, which is a more receptive act. Moreover, contexts are provided in two of the reading tests (oral reading and silent reading comprehension), whereas in writing the children must produce their own contexts. Thus, grammar and language awareness may be less important for reading than for writing. Vocabulary, however, seems to have a strong influence on both reading and writing, according to the factor analyses.

Factor analyses performed for each separate grade confirmed the findings from the analyses for the total population reported above. Generally, two main factors were found for the reading, writing, and language measures: a meaning factor (for example, content in writing, word meanings, reading comprehension) and a precision factor (for example, word recognition, spelling, form in writing). In the early grades (2 and 3), reading, writing, and language tended to be global; that is, children who had high or low scores on some reading and writing measures had similarly high or low scores on other reading or writing measures. For grades 2 and 3, two reading factors emerged: word recognition and word meaning, with the former more prominent than the latter. In the later elementary grades, the meaning factor took on greater importance than the recognition factor. These findings again confirm the research that spans more than 70 years on the critical importance for beginning reading of word recognition and decoding (Chall, 1967, 1983a, 1983b, 1989; Perfetti, 1985; Adams, 1989; Juel, 1988).

The two factors we found for writing were similar to those for reading: form and precision with words (which resemble word recognition in reading) and content (which resembles meaning in reading). Viewing the writing factors as similar to the reading factors can permit greater insight into the writing patterns of our population. Generally, their content and ideas (meaning) in both narration and exposition were better than their form (precision). Shaughnessy (1977) essentially found the same thing in her now classic study of the writing of poor urban college students, whom she called "basic writers"; their greatest need was in the domain of form, not content. Our various writing analyses—qualitative and quantitative—showed that our population of low-income children lacked knowledge of form and structure (for example, organization, syntax) and facility with some tasks requiring word precision (such as spelling and handwriting). They also lacked words with which to express themselves, as was shown by their use of only a very limited number of words beyond the commonest thousand in the English language. This lack of knowledge of less common words was found also on the vocabulary tests in the reading and language batteries.

Developmental Trends in Reading, Writing, and Language

Overall, the developmental trends for reading, writing, and language were quite similar. On most measures of reading, writing, and language, development was greater in the earlier than in the later grades. On most tests, the greatest gains were made from grade 2 to grade 3, lesser gains from 4 to 5, and least from 6 to 7. These trends held for the reading tests and for most of the writing and language measures.

The trends also held for both the above-average and the below-average readers. The below-average readers differed from the above-average ones and from the total group mainly with regard to the time when the deceleration started and its intensity: the below-average readers began to decelerate earlier, and their deceleration was more intense. Overall, word meaning scores decelerated earliest for the entire group, as did the reading tests that did not provide context (such as word recognition and spelling). The two "contextual" tests (oral reading of connected passages and silent reading comprehension) held up longest.

A weakness in vocabulary was found in the writing and the language measures as well as in reading. Beginning in fourth grade, the words on the vocabulary tests (the word meaning test on the reading battery) become less common, more abstract, more literary, and longer. To function on grade level, that is, to be able to read and understand the textbooks and other materials written for these grades, considerable growth in a more difficult and abstract vocabulary would have to take place after grade 3. Evidently, such growth was not taking place in our population of students.

Conclusions

Our study of the reading, writing, and language development of these students was based on the assumption that, if lags exist in literacy and language, then a knowledge of the nature and extent of the lags would help suggest ways to lessen or overcome them (both in school and in the home and community). The questions we raised were: How do literacy and language develop among children of low-income families, especially in the middle years? How is their reading development related to language and writing development? Is their literacy and language development different from that of the larger, normative population, and, if so, what may explain these differences?

Our findings indicate that the low-income children in our sample demonstrated many strengths in literacy and language, particularly in the first three grades of elementary school. In the primary grades, they differed little from a normative population. It was the fourth graders who started to lose ground and fall behind, especially the below-average readers. The above-average readers, although they tended to score on or above grade level up to grade 6 or 7 on most of the reading tests, showed signs of falling behind in these grades on some tests, suggesting that they might continue to do so at an increasing rate in later grades (see the section on follow-up in Chapter 3). Thus, both the below-average and the above-average readers followed the pattern of development commonly reported in the research literature and in reports of school districts for low-income children:

performance on grade level in the earlier grades but performance below grade level in later elementary grades.

How are these developmental patterns related to the experiences these children had at home and in school? Can their patterns of development be influenced for the better at home or school? Can the deceleration be prevented? These questions will be discussed in the chapters that follow.

7

Classroom Instruction and Literacy Environments

Do some classroom methods, materials, and procedures have more beneficial effects on the literacy and language development of low-income children than others? To investigate this question, members of the research team systematically observed the classrooms of the children in the sample and interviewed their teachers. They then related this information to the children's reading and language achievement. In this chapter, we present findings from those analyses most useful for improving theories and research of literacy and language development.*

First, we present the findings on classroom and school factors in relation to two tests from the reading battery—word recognition and silent reading comprehension—and the vocabulary knowledge subtest from the WISC-R. The three tests were selected to represent the major factors in reading found in the factor analyses and developmental analyses reported in the previous chapter—language, cognition, and reading skills. We then present the classroom effects—separately by the lower and by the higher grades. The goal was to relate the children's gains in word recognition, silent reading comprehension, and vocabulary during one year of instruction (from May of the first year to May of the second year of the study) to aspects of their classroom environment. More specifically, the focus was on class-

*This chapter is based on the more extensive and detailed report by Jean Chandler and Lowry Hemphill, *Models of Classrooms as Effective Literacy Environments for Low-Income Children,* conducted under a Graduate Research in Education Award from the Association of American Publishers, Harvard Graduate School of Education, October 1983. The interpretations presented here, however, are our own.

room characteristics which produced gains greater than one year for each of the three measures.

Information on the characteristics of the classrooms (for example, teaching procedures, materials, and methods) came from several sources: observations of reading lessons, observers' ratings for each classroom, teachers' questionnaires, and interview responses. Table 7-1 (from Chandler and Hemphill, 1983) gives details about each classroom characteristic. Most of these characteristics were found to be good predictors of reading achievement in the research literature (Chall, 1986, 1987).

Each child was observed in each of three classroom contexts: a reading lesson, whole-group instruction in some subject area, and independent work. Written narratives of the child-focused observations of reading lessons were coded *post hoc* for the presence or absence of a number of factors, including use of structured materials, substantial oral reading, and explicit teaching of word attack, comprehension, and vocabulary.

Because lessons in language arts and other subjects (such as social studies and science) are also relevant to reading growth, observers rated the overall instructional quality and literacy environment for each classroom. These ratings were based on all the observations done in a particular classroom (including ethnographic notes of informal visits, lists of materials, and maps of the classroom as well as the child-focused narratives of formal observations).

Teachers responded to written questions about their instructional practices in reading and writing, particularly to the kind of reading instruction each focal child received. The teachers' questionnaires consisted of open-ended questions as well as checklists and questions requiring only a yes/no or a numerical answer. In response to the questionnaire, teachers provided information on the following: time allocated for reading instruction; the focus of instruction in reading lessons; materials used in reading; the degree of teachers' direction in lessons; type of homework; and student attendance. The teachers noted the textbook each child used in reading lessons, and the text's published readability level was compared to each focal child's tested reading level.

Effects of Classroom Factors

From the variety of classroom and teaching measures obtained, four variables were selected for particular emphasis: structure of the class-

Table 7-1 Sources and definitions of variables

From classroom observations of reading lessons:

- *Exclusive use of basals or workbooks.* Children did not use materials other than texts or workbooks from published basal reading series during the reading lesson observed.
- *Substantial oral reading.* Children read aloud from a reading text or other print materials for at least half of the 30-minute reading lesson observed.
- *Explicit word attack instruction.* The teacher explained or demonstrated a strategy for pronouncing unfamiliar words (e.g., said "There's a silent letter in that word") during the reading lesson observed.
- *Inference questioning.* The teacher asked students a question that required making an inference from the text (e.g., asked "What do you think might happen next?") during the reading lesson observed.
- *Relating reading to content areas.* The teacher explained or demonstrated how a reading skill could be applied to learning content in other school subjects such as English, social studies, or science (e.g., after students had practiced finding main ideas in reading workbook passages, the teacher said "This is the same thing you do when you make an outline in social studies class").
- *Explicit comprehension instruction.* The teacher explained or demonstrated a strategy for deriving meaning from text (e.g., the teacher showed that quotation marks set off reported speech from description in a narrative) during the reading lesson observed.
- *Explicit vocabulary instruction.* The teacher either told students the meaning of an unfamiliar word or helped them derive the definition themselves through techniques like discussion, use of glossary or dictionary.

From observer ratings:

- *Quality of instruction.* Rating of overall quality of instruction in terms of level of challenge and involvement for student, orderliness, amount of explicit instruction.
- *Literacy environment.* Rating of overall environment for language and literacy development in terms of access to a variety of print and other materials, use of library, frequency of writing activities.
- *Observers' rating of overall quality of instruction*
  - *positive:* teacher regularly gives explanations, develops concepts; children have routines, classroom is orderly without being tense; most children seem challenged or involved; organization may range from open to traditional.
  - *neutral:* teacher sometimes gives explanations or develops concepts; some evidence of routines; children lack stimulating activities.
  - *negative:* teacher rarely gives explanations or develops concepts; chaotic and/or rigid atmosphere; heavy emphasis on discipline (not always effective); many children seem bored or alienated.
- *Observers' rating of the classroom as a literacy environment*
  - *enriched:* varied reading materials; frequent library visits; frequent creative and expository writing assignments; physical environment includes resources beyond texts; displays of student work.
  - *average:* standard instruction, following a basal text and workbook; some variety in reading materials; some library visits; occasional writing assignments; some posting of student work.

Table 7-1 (continued)

impoverished: little variety in reading materials; infrequent use of library; teacher does not organize writing activities; physical environment bleak and largely limited to texts; no display of student work.

From teacher questionnaire responses:

- *Teacher-directed lessons.* Teacher's estimate of the proportion of time when she, rather than the students, "directs activities and selects materials" in all types of lessons.
- *Field trips.* Number of different types of class field trips reported on checklist.
- *Library visits.* Number of class visits to the library reported by the teacher.
- *Workbook homework.* Teacher's report of typically assigning workbook or worksheet homework for reading class, rather than reading or writing assignments.
- *Trade books.* Teacher's report of using "trade" books (e.g., paperbacks, library books) for reading instruction on a checklist of different materials.
- *Types of materials.* Number of different types of materials teacher reported using to teach reading on a checklist including basals, basal workshops, skills workbooks, trade books, teacher-written stories and exercises, games.
- *Critical thinking emphasis.* Teacher's inclusion of "critical thinking/reasoning" on a checklist of reading skills emphasized with the class (checklist also included word attack, literal comprehension, vocabulary, study skills, speed reading).
- *Creative writing.* Teacher's mention of "creative writing" in her description of the types of writing activities students engaged in.
- *Book reports.* Teacher's mention of book reports as a type of writing students engaged in.
- *Writing frequency.* Teacher's report of frequency of writing activities (on a scale from "every day" to "less than once a month").
- *Difficulty level of reading text.* A comparison of the publisher's grade level rating (e.g., 3.5, 6.0) of the main text each child used in reading lessons with the child's tested reading level on the standardized reading comprehension test administered the previous spring.
- *Text completion.* Teacher's report of how much of the child's main reading text was completed by the end of the academic year (on a scale from "less than half" to "fully completed").
- *Allocated time for reading instruction.* The number of times each child had a reading lesson each week multiplied by the average length of the lesson (on a scale from 15 to 60+ minutes), both from teacher's reports.
- *Single skills emphasis.* Teacher's affirmative response to the question, "Is there a single skill or group of skills you've emphasized for the target child or his/her reading group this year?"
- *Comprehension emphasis.* Teacher's mention of comprehension in her description of the single skill or group of skills emphasized for the target child in reading lesson.
- *Vocabulary emphasis.* Teacher's mention of vocabulary in her description of the single skill or group of skills emphasized for the target child in reading lesson.
- *Student attendance.* Number of days each child was present in school according to teacher reports.

room instruction, higher-level processes (that is, the amount of focus on reading comprehension), challenge (level of difficulty), and enrichment (reading outside of textbooks and workbooks). These variables were related to the two measures of reading (word recognition and reading comprehension) and to one of language (vocabulary).

Structure

Table 7-2* presents the correlations of classroom variables related to structure (with the three reading and vocabulary measures). The table shows that specific classroom practices falling within the structure variable (either observed or reported by the teachers) relate differently to gains in the two reading measures and to vocabulary. Gains in word recognition were significantly related to the classroom conditions of workbook homework and students' attendance. The exclusive use of a basal reader, a workbook, or both also correlated positively, although not quite significantly, with word recognition gains.

The classroom factors that were strongest in predicting reading comprehension gains were "allocated time for reading instruction" (the more time the better), "explicit comprehension instruction" (for example, the teacher explained or demonstrated a strategy for deriving meaning from a text), and workbook homework (also significantly

Table 7-2 Correlation coefficients for "structure" variables, whole population

Classroom factors	Word recognition gain	Reading comprehension gain	Vocabulary gain
Reading lesson observations			
Exclusive use of basal readers and workbook	.26	.10	−.48[a]
Explicit comprehension instruction	−.06	.39[b]	.14
Teacher reports			
Teacher-directed lessons	−.10	−.23	.09
Workbook homework	.32[b]	.39[b]	.14
Difficulty level of reading text	.17	.28	.56[b]
Allocated time for reading instruction	−.03	.41[b]	−.09
Single skills emphasis	−.23	−.02	.22
Student attendance	.32[b]	.13	−.10

**Source*: Adapted from Chandler and Hemphill, 1983.
a. $p < .01$.
b. $p < .05$.

correlated with gains in word recognition). Vocabulary gains were most strongly associated with less exclusive use of basal readers and workbooks and the use of more difficult textbooks.

These findings are reminiscent of the factor analyses and other analyses of the students' scores reported earlier for reading (Chapter 6). Essentially, there seem to be at least two broad factors in reading and language—a meaning factor (word meaning and reading comprehension) and a recognition factor (word recognition)—and different classroom conditions seem to have different influences on each of these factors. Some classroom conditions seem to produce greater gains in word recognition (for example, use of basal readers and workbooks), while others seem to produce greater gains in reading comprehension and vocabulary (meaning) (for example, explicit instruction, more time for practice, and use of more difficult texts).

Overall, gains in word recognition were associated more with structured activities—attendance, workbook homework, exclusive use of basal readers and workbooks. Not one of these classroom conditions, however, was related positively to vocabulary gains. The two factors that were related to gains in vocabulary concerned greater challenge; that is, only harder and more varied materials resulted in vocabulary gains. This suggests that the best way to help these children grow in word meanings is to expand the curriculum and make it more challenging.

The effects of structure by grades and by above-average and below-average readers suggest further insights. First, what seems to be effective for reading and vocabulary development in the lower grades may not be effective in the later grades. For example, a single-skills emphasis (that is, less variety in practice) was beneficial for third graders' word recognition but had a negative relation with seventh graders' word recognition gains. Similarly, although focused reading instruction produced greater gains in comprehension among the younger children, it did not produce expected gains among seventh graders. In addition, seventh graders in classes with a high level of teacher direction of activities and selection of materials had lower gains in reading comprehension compared to seventh graders in classes where more freedom of choice of materials and activities was found.

Second, the findings support the view that the development of different reading components is affected differently by various classroom conditions. For example, explicit instruction in comprehension, which produced gains in reading comprehension, did not seem to produce gains in word recognition or in vocabulary. "Allocated time for reading instruction" was related positively to gains in reading comprehension, at all grade levels and for both above-average and below-average readers, but not for word recognition and vocabulary. "Difficulty level of texts" produced strong gains in vocabulary but weaker gains in comprehension, and practically none in word recognition.

For vocabulary development, the exclusive use of basal readers and workbooks did not have a positive effect on the reading gains of children in the lower or higher grades. The limited level of difficulty of the readers and workbooks probably did not allow for a broad enough exposure to the meanings of more difficult words. (See, in this connection, Chall, Conard, and Harris, 1977; Chall, Conard, and Harris-Sharples, 1983).

To illustrate the findings on the influence of structure on reading achievement, we present some observations of a third-grade classroom (Chall, Snow, et al., 1982). In this third-grade classroom, the observers noted that the teacher was businesslike and task-oriented, as were the children. During the reading lesson, the teacher was observed using the teacher's guide to the basal reader to check systematically the children's reading comprehension. The reading lesson consisted of a review of the part of a story that the children had read previously; silent reading, followed by answering questions; and oral reading, followed by "sounding" and then defining polysyllabic and other difficult words.

The spelling lesson focused on silent letters. The teacher wrote words on the blackboard; students read them in unison; and individual students circled silent letters in the spelling words and defined the words. The teacher then erased the words, and the students spelled them from memory. The activity closed with a spelling test.

The materials used in the observed lessons were from either textbooks or workbooks. The materials on the shelves also tended to be text materials—three different basal reading textbooks on three levels of difficulty and a variety of workbooks for reading, phonics, spelling, language and grammar, mathematics, and health. Non-textbook materials included enough elementary dictionaries for each child and games such as Scrabble and Quizmo.

Thus, the third-grade classroom observed reflected a strong sense of structure and organization; these are characteristics that were shown to be associated with greater gains in word recognition and comprehension than in word meaning. Overall, in terms of the reading stages, this third-grade class focused on those components most important for the early grades—word recognition and comprehension—and focused less on word meanings, more important in later grades. Although the lesson could be characterized by some "higher-level processes" (a focus on reading comprehension), challenge, and enrichment, the major characteristic of this classroom seemed to be structure.

Instruction in Higher-Level Processes

The higher-level instructional processes included such activities as comprehension and vocabulary (for example, whether reading lessons included inference questions, demonstrated ways of understanding a text, related reading to the subject areas, or gave explicit instruction in the meanings of words). Included in this category was a rating of the overall classroom literacy environment ("stimulating activities" and "varied reading materials" were evidence of a good literacy environment). Teachers' emphases on higher-level skills were also included in the category, determined by their answers to the questionnaires and especially their own description of their instructional emphases (for instance, "critical/thinking/reasoning," study skills).

Table 7-3* presents the correlations of higher-level processes with two reading variables (word recognition and comprehension) and a language variable (vocabulary). The striking feature of this table is that there are few significant effects. Overall, for the higher-level

Table 7-3 Correlation coefficients for "higher level" instructional variables

Classroom factors	Word recognition gain	Reading comprehension gain	Vocabulary gain
Reading lesson observations			
Inference questioning	−.27	.14	.25
Relating reading to content areas	−.23	−.10	.15
No substantial oral reading	−.14	.03	.14
Observer ratings			
Literacy environment	−.33[a]	.22	.36[a]
Teacher reports			
Emphasis on critical thinking	−.33[a]	−.01	.19
Emphasis on comprehension	−.15	−.16	.26
Emphasis on vocabulary	−.11	.01	−.07

**Source*: Adapted from Chandler and Hemphill, 1983.
a. $p < .05$.

processes, we could find only one significant positive relationship: "literacy environment" (that is, classrooms that had "stimulating activities" and "varied reading materials") was associated with gains in vocabulary. Two significant negative relationships were found for word recognition: both a "literacy environment" and an "emphasis on critical reading" produced lower than expected gains in word recognition. Thus, it would seem that the richer the literacy environment, the higher are the vocabulary gains, but the lower are the word recognition gains. How could a rich literacy environment be related to low gains in word recognition? It is possible that teachers who create rich literacy environments pay less attention to word recognition than they do to higher-order processes; or it may be, as we found for structure, that word recognition benefits from more structured activities such as the use of basal readers and workbooks and regular practice (which may be related to regular attendance); or all of these may have an impact.

We find more positive effects for higher-level processes when we divide the population into those in the earlier or in the higher grades, and into the above-average and below-average readers. Overall, as would be expected, those in the higher grades seemed to benefit more from emphasis on the higher-level processes. For example, in comprehension, there were significant gains for those seventh graders who received more inference questioning and whose teachers related reading to the subject areas. Fifth graders made significantly higher vocabulary gains when their teachers emphasized inference questioning, and the above-average readers (but not the below-average) learned more word meanings from a rich literacy environment.

These findings are in accordance with those of a recent meta-analysis of research on teaching metacognitive processes for reading comprehension (Haller, Child, and Walberg, 1988). It found that positive effects of teaching metacognition (higher-level processes) begin to appear only in the seventh to eighth grades, not earlier. Both findings tend to confirm the model of reading development on which our study is based—that higher-level comprehension processes begin at about Stage 3B (reading grade levels 7 and 8), when the materials read require more critical analysis.

To illustrate the classroom characteristics of higher-level processes, enrichment, and challenge, we present below observations from one of the fourth-grade classes in our study.

The classroom contained a wealth of materials, including textbooks, workbooks, more than 600 books (mostly paperbacks), comics, games, dictionaries, and encyclopedias. The activities observed combined traditional instruction from textbooks and workbooks with writing opportunities and with reading of trade books—which challenged the children intellectually and imaginatively. Word meanings were a part of all lessons observed. Wall charts focused on new words, and the teacher read aloud novels each day. An observed math lesson focused on the meanings of such words as square, pentagon, and rectangle. The teacher also provided knowledge (about Roman numerals, planets, French painters, and famous people) that was unfamiliar to the daily experience of the students.

Thus, the observers gave this fourth-grade class high ratings on all the four characteristics: structure, higher-level skills, enrichment, and challenge. These characteristics are particularly important in grade 4 when the language and cognitive needs for reading development become greater than they were in the primary grades and when vocabulary demands upon the reader increase.

Extent of Challenge

Extent of challenge concerns the difficulty of the reading materials in relation to the reading ability of the reader. The more difficult the material in relation to student ability, the greater is the challenge. Table 7-4* presents correlations for extent of challenge in relation to gains in word recognition, reading comprehension, and vocabulary. For challenge, we used one measure: the relationship between the level of difficulty of the reading text and the reading ability of the student.

What is striking about the "challenge" variable is its positive influence on all three measures. Challenge was one of the most potent predictors of a significant gain in meaning vocabulary; indeed, the correlation of challenge with vocabulary gains is the highest of any classroom or teaching factor. Although not quite significant, challenge was also positively related to comprehension and word recognition.

Table 7-4 Correlation coefficients for "challenge" variable

	Word recognition gain	Reading comprehension gain	Vocabulary gain
Difficulty level of reading text	.31	.25	.57[a]

**Source*: Adapted from Chandler and Hemphill, 1983.
a. $p < .05$.

The effects of a challenging level of difficulty were especially strong for the below-average readers—on word recognition and comprehension. These findings are similar to those of an earlier study of textbook difficulty in relation to SAT verbal scores, where the use of more difficult texts, particularly in the first grade, tended to be associated with higher SAT scores (Chall, Conard, and Harris, 1977).

These findings suggest a reconsideration of the general policy of assigning easy materials for reading instruction, especially to the poorest readers. Chall, Conard, and Harris-Sharples (1983), for example, found that instructional materials on or above the students' tested reading level produce more positive effects. This also fits with Vygotsky's contention (1962) that instruction is most effective if it precedes rather than follows development; that is, instruction should be at the child's "zone of proximal development," that level at which he can learn from a teacher or peer.

Enrichment

In this study, we considered enrichment to refer to a variety of print materials and instructional activities. Among the variables classified as "enriching" from the teachers' reports were field trips, library visits, use of trade books, and assignment of reading and writing homework. Table 7-5* presents the correlation coefficients between the enrichment variable and gains in word recognition, reading comprehension, and vocabulary.

The most striking feature of the correlations is that enrichment is frequently negatively related to reading comprehension and word

Table 7-5 Correlation coefficients for "enrichment" variables, whole population

Teacher reports	Word recognition gain	Reading comprehension gain	Vocabulary gain
Field trips	−.05	−.26	−.04
Library visits	−.04	.39[a]	.16
Reading and writing homework	−.32[a]	−.39[a]	−.14
Trade books	−.18	−.14	.23
Types of materials	−.03	.40[a]	.26
Creative writing	−.40[a]	−.13	.21
Book reports	.06	−.13	−.11
Writing frequency	−.35[a]	−.06	.06

**Source*: Adapted from Chandler and Hemphill, 1983.
a. $p < .05$.

recognition gains. Word recognition was especially negatively related to enrichment of writing activities (for example, reading and writing homework, creative writing, and writing frequency). Perhaps the correlations are negative because the children's writing was found to be deficient in less familiar words (see Chapter 4). Thus, the more time the children spent writing (that is, using only the commonest words), the less time they had to practice recognizing less familiar words.

Few significant effects on reading comprehension were found for the enrichment variables; those with the strongest effects were library visits and variety of reading materials for instruction. More of the enrichment variables were related positively to vocabulary gains; the use of trade books, use of a variety of types of materials, and creative writing were especially related.

One could make a distinction between enrichment approaches that expand children's access to reading materials (for example, library visits and use of a variety of types of materials in reading lessons) and enrichment approaches that introduce more varied activities (such as field trips and creative writing). If so, "access" enrichment variables (that is, direct experience with enriched materials) exhibit several positive and significant correlations and show smaller negative effects with gains in comprehension. "Activity" enrichment variables, on the other hand, show consistently negative correlations with gains in comprehension and exhibit a mixture of positive and negative relationships with vocabulary development.

To illustrate how critical all four characteristics—structure, higher-level skills, enrichment, and challenge—are in the later grades, we present excerpts from observations made in one of the sixth-grade classes in our study.

The purpose of the lesson observed was to prepare the students to read a story in their basal reader; the lesson focused on the meanings of 33 new words in the story. The teacher listed the words on the board, asked for meanings, supplied about a third of the words' meanings, and then directed students to look up definitions in the dictionary for homework. Having spent the entire class on word meanings, the students had only a few minutes to begin to read the text before the bell rang.

The strongest characteristic of this classroom was structure; however, the structure constrained the lesson, which lacked balance; it gave too much attention to word meanings and too little time to read. There was very little evidence of features other than structure. Although the teaching of word meanings falls within the "higher-level processes" category, the teacher relied mainly on having students define words without also having them focus on the use of those words in varied contexts. The tasks observed could not be considered challenging; although the textbook was grade-appropriate, it was below the level of about half the students in the class. Finally, there was little evidence of enrichment; there were no trade books in the classroom.

The three illustrations provided above—one each from a third-grade, a fourth-grade, and a sixth-grade classroom—indicate the varying importance of the four characteristics of structure, higher-level skills, enrichment, and challenge for instruction and learning at all levels. All four characteristics are particularly important in grades 4 and beyond, when the reading task demands higher language and cognitive development and thus is influenced more than in the early grades by instruction in higher-level processes, enrichment, and challenge.

Summary

The four kinds of classroom variables tend to have different effects on word recognition, reading comprehension, and meaning vocabulary. Thus, word recognition seems to benefit most from classroom "structure" and "challenge" (difficult texts). Reading comprehension is also positively associated with "structure" (explicit comprehension instruction and allocated time for reading instruction) and with "enrichment" (library visits and a variety of materials). Vocabulary is most influenced by "challenge" (difficulty level of reading text), "higher-level" instruction (literacy environment), and some aspects of "enrichment" (trade books, variety of materials).

These findings generally confirm the analyses reported earlier on the patterns of development for reading, writing, and language (see Chapters 3, 4, and 5) and the factor analyses (see Chapter 6). Specifically, all these analyses confirm that word recognition, word meanings, and reading comprehension are separate aspects of literacy; what fosters development in one does not necessarily foster growth in the other. Word recognition in reading, as well as form in writing, spelling, and grammar, benefit from structured, direct teaching that is challenging. Overall, the various analyses showed that higher-level instruction and enrichment factors had only negative, if any, effect on word recognition gains. Reading comprehension, since it requires

precision in both word recognition and meaning, developed well with structure, and it also benefited from higher-level instruction and enrichment. Meaning vocabulary was fostered by challenging texts and by higher-level instruction and enrichment factors.

8

Home Influences on Literacy and Language

The families in our study, all classified as low-income, reflected the great diversity of the community in which we conducted our research.* Our sample included two-parent and single-parent families; families in which a second language was spoken; parents who were school dropouts and some who had attended college; and highly organized families as well as those in which routines seemed to vary from one day to the next. There were homes where parents read regularly to their children and homes where children regularly spent their free time in front of the television.

The families in the study shared many similarities. Most were quite stable; 68 percent were two-parent families. More than two-thirds had lived in the same residence for more than three years, and half had maintained the same home for more than five years. The families resided in several different sections of the community, and many of the parents still lived in the same neighborhood where they had grown up. Most children had regular contacts with members of their extended families; only two had no siblings. Nearly all of the parents in our sample wanted and expected their children to complete more education than they had themselves. Seventy percent of the mothers hoped their children would attend college; the remainder hoped their children would graduate from high school.

The data presented in this chapter are drawn from in-depth interviews with parents and children and from an observer rating scale. We focus only on those areas that had possible effects on literacy. Specifically, we focus on the family and home influences on literacy

*This chapter is based on material originally reported in *Families and Literacy* (Chall, Snow, et al., 1982) and further analyzed and discussed by Snow et al. in *Unfulfilled Expectations* (in press).

and language development (see Chall, Snow, et al., 1982; Snow et al., forthcoming). These influences are grouped under three broad categories: the family's provision for literacy and language; the organization of the home and its human relationships; and the contacts between the family and the school.

Provision of Literacy Environment by the Family

Homes were classified as providing strong literacy environments if parents provided literary experiences to the children by reading to them, buying them books, teaching them to read, and expressing high educational expectations for them. Also included under strong literacy environments were homes where the parents had attained high levels of education and read a variety of difficult reading materials.

Generally, parental provision of a strong literacy environment in the home was positively associated with the children's literacy and language development; it was strongly associated with language (word meanings) and also significantly associated with reading. The strongest specific predictors of both reading and vocabulary knowledge were literacy environment in the home, mother's education, mother's educational expectations for the child, and father's education.

Overall, the mothers affected the literacy and language development of their children more than the fathers. This is not surprising, since the mothers typically spent more time with the children than did the fathers. They, more than the fathers, helped with homework, selected reading materials, answered questions, read bedtime stories, enforced television rules, and supported learning in other ways. The mother's achievement and interest in literacy were also significantly correlated with reading development. The child's reading development was positively related to the number of authors the mother mentioned by name in response to questions that investigated their past and present interests in reading (such as "Who are your favorite authors?" "Who were your favorite authors when you were a child?"). Chomsky (1972) found similar associations for a middle-class population. When the middle-class mothers expressed stronger preferences for reading and had greater recall of their childhood favorites, their children also had more highly developed language and reading achievement.

Also significantly related to both language and reading were the number of activities parents engaged in outside of work (such as social clubs, church groups, and union groups). Perhaps those who are more involved in such activities have a broader world view, reflected in their language and literacy interests. Indeed, Marston (1982) found that those upper elementary and junior high school students who were more involved in out-of-school activities read more widely than those who were less involved.

Organization of the Family

Are factors such as extent of family organization, stress, and the warmth of human relationships in the home related to the students' language and literacy development? Do "organized families" (as compared to those less organized) make a greater contribution to their children's literacy development? Does a supportive climate in the home—one in which the children develop self-confidence and a positive self-image—contribute to literacy achievement? Does a supportive climate in the home lead to positive expectations on the part of children about their relations with teachers and other adults, to success following persistence at difficult tasks, to setting goals and regulating their behavior—characteristics of a good school learner? The basic assumption behind the possible contribution of family organization is that homes may either enhance or hamper children's ability to function at school, depending upon the degree of stress or supportiveness in the home.

The three major groupings of variables used to measure the "organized family" were:

1. Measures of organization in the family (for example, physical neatness, cleanliness, rules of behavior, scheduling).
2. Measures of emotional climate (for example, children's views of their relationships with parents, extent of punitive or nurturant behavior by parents).
3. Measures of stress (for example, financial stress, life changes).

Overall, these organizational and affective factors were positively and significantly related to reading and language development. However, the correlations were lower than for the home as a provider of literacy. The strongest relationship between family organization and gains in reading and language was found for "frequency of outings with adults." Overall, it appears from the nature of the correlations that a home's cognitive characteristics are more influential for a student's literacy and language development than are its affective characteristics. Although these differences may be influenced by our sample, we suggest that they are more general and that they may be explained by the fact that both reading and vocabulary are cognitive tasks that require learning. The families that provided stronger literacy environments were similar to the classrooms that produced stronger gains in reading and language; they provided more stimulating and challenging environments for the children's reading and vocabulary development. Although a more organized and less stressful home may enhance a child's motivation for learning to read, it does not directly provide the opportunity to develop and learn the skills related to language and reading development. In fact, most stress variables (for example, the financial and emotional stress of the parents) had close to zero correlation with the language and reading measures.

Contacts between Family and School

There is much emphasis on the importance of family-school collaboration in current educational reforms. In our study, we wished to find out the extent of home-school collaboration and whether it influenced the literacy and language development of the students. We were concerned with several kinds of parent-school collaboration:

1. Parental involvement with the school (for example, joining the PTA and similar organizations, serving as a volunteer classroom aide, accompanying classes on trips and outings).
2. The frequency of parental contacts with teachers (for example, visiting the school and teacher with regard to the child's academic progress).
3. The child's regular and punctual attendance.
4. Homework help (for example, the school informing parents of what children are learning in school, parents helping the child with homework).
5. The nature and quality of parent-child interaction during homework.

Overall, parent-school collaboration related positively to the children's reading, writing, and vocabulary development. The variable that was most significantly related to literacy and language development was parental involvement with the school (for example, the frequency with which the mother or father attended PTA meetings, class meetings, school-related committees, school concerts, or special programs and helped in class or with field trips). Attendance and punctuality in school were also related positively to reading development: the students with better attendance made greater gains, particularly in word recognition. This again shows the importance of being in school (that is, being exposed to instruction) in order to learn what is perhaps the most specific, teachable aspect of literacy—word recognition. As we observed in Chapter 7, word recognition is also most highly related to structure and challenge. Thus, those who attend school less regularly may not learn as many words because they do not receive enough instruction and challenge.

Parental assistance with homework did not, on the whole, have strong effects on literacy and language development, nor did the frequency of homework assignments. However, the children who were assigned worksheets for homework had significantly higher gains in reading than did the children who received general reading and writing assignments. This relation may have come from the fact that it was the younger children who received such homework, and it is generally the younger children who gain from more structured reading tasks (see Chapters 7 and 9). Another aspect of homework that had positive effects on reading development was promptness and consistency of turning in homework: significantly more above-average than below-average readers turned in their homework consistently and on time.

In sum, neither frequency of homework assignments nor getting help with homework at home was related to gains on literacy measures. Receiving direct assignments (on worksheets) and doing homework consistently and on time did distinguish the above-average from the below-average readers. Consistency in completing homework was positively related to family organization, teachers' judgments about the family's contributions to the child's school success, and the teacher's expectations for the child.

Report Cards: What Do They Reflect?

When they compared the children's report card grades for reading and writing with their scores on various tests, Snow et al. found that their grades did not consistently reflect their test scores. During the first year of the study, nearly three-quarters of the children received A's and B's for reading on their report cards. It was not just the above-average readers who received good grades; more than half of the below-average students also received high grades (A's or B's) for reading on their report cards (Snow et al., in press, pp. 163–164). It may well be that the teachers graded the students on the gains they made during the year rather than on their level of achievement. If so, the mothers seemed to be unaware of this. In fact, when asked whether their children were reading above grade level, 68 percent of the mothers in our study thought that they were. Thus, many mothers thought their children were reading better than their test performance indicated.

Parent-Teacher Conferences

Parent-teacher contacts, whether initiated by the teacher or the parent, were positively correlated with teachers' perceptions of the home's contribution to the child's learning. Teacher-parent contacts were also correlated with higher expectations by the teacher of the child's educational achievement, and with gains in the child's reading. Below-average readers whose families were contacted about academic concerns were more likely to make substantial gains in reading. Parents who initiated contacts learned ways to assist with homework and learned about the child's current reading achievement. Such contacts, by signaling the importance of the child's schooling to the parents, seemed also to modify the teacher's assessments of the child's abilities and prospects.

Overall, the teachers' expectations of pupils' learning seemed to decline in the successive school grades: the teachers' expectations were highest in the early grades and lowest in the sixth and seventh grades. The families of the sixth and seventh grade students made the fewest contacts with the school, and these were also the grades in which the children made the lowest gains per year and the grades in which their scores were farthest from national norms. Thus, we find that teacher expectations and school-family contacts go through a decline in the later elementary grades similar to the slump in students' reading and language achievement.

In sum, among the parent-school partnership variables, we found that children's attendance, regular and prompt completion of homework, and teacher-parent contacts were positively related to literacy. Teachers' expectations of student achievement and extent of teacher-parent contacts seemed to be lowest in the sixth and seventh grades, as were the students' literacy and language scores when compared with expected achievement.

Relationship of Home to School Factors

Goodman and Hemphill classified children in the study as having strong advantages from home or strong advantages from school (Hemphill and Goodman, 1982; Goodman and Hemphill, 1982). They found that those who were fortunate in both made the greatest gains in literacy and language in one year. Those who had an advantage in only one setting—whether in the home or in school—made the next higher gains. Those who had no strong advantages in either home or school made the least gains.

Tables 8-1 and 8-2 give additional details about the children's experiences in the home and in school (Snow et al., in press). Table 8-1 presents the children's school experiences (whether favorable or unfavorable) in relation to their gains in reading achievement, for the first and second years of the study; Table 8-2 relates the home characteristics (rated "high" or "low") to gains in reading achievement.

Table 8-1 shows that when schools provided positive experiences in two consecutive years, 100 percent of the children made good gains in reading achievement. When the students had one good school year and one weak, 60 percent made good gains in reading achievement, while 40 percent did not. However, when children experienced two "bad" years in school, only 38 percent made adequate gains in achievement; 62 percent did not.

Table 8-2 shows that the relationship of home influences to reading achievement is essentially similar to that for school influences. For those whose homes received high ratings, 87 percent made good gains, while only 13 percent did not. For those children whose homes received low ratings, only about one-third achieved well; two-thirds achieved below expectations.

Table 8-1 School rating and gains in reading achievement

			Significant relationship to reading achievement			
			More than a year's gain		Less than a year's gain	
Number of students	Rating first year	Rating second year	Number	%	Number	%
5	High	High	5	100	0	0
15	Low	High	9	60	6	40
8	Low	Low	3	38	5	62

Table 8-2 Home rating and gains in reading achievement

Number of students	Rating	Gains in reading achievement: More than a year's gain — Number	%	Less than a year's gain — Number	%
15	High	13	87	2	13
13	Low	4	31	9	69

Snow and her colleagues argue that the effects of inadequate support for literacy in the home or in the school could be counteracted by high support in the other area. However, this seemed to occur only when the classroom or the home provided a very strong literacy environment to overcome the weaknesses of the other. On the whole, the home seems to be less able to compensate for poor schooling, particularly at the upper elementary grades. Thus the role of the school may ultimately be more central than that of the home, especially for the older children.

9

Influences on the Lower and Higher Grades

To what extent are the school and home influences on literacy and language similar across the grades? The developmental model of reading that underlies our study, as well as the findings already reported, suggest that some kinds of school experiences are more effective in the earlier grades and less effective in later grades, and vice versa. Are there also differential effects for the home influences? That is, are some home influences especially effective for students in the earlier or in the later elementary grades? Are some home and school factors more important at certain stages of reading development? Are there shifts with development in the relative influences of home and school?

The relevance of these questions can be appreciated when we consider the effects of reading to children on the development of their language and literacy. There is general consensus among teachers and parents that reading to children is beneficial, and this has considerable research confirmation (Chomsky, 1972; Anderson et al., 1985), but one wonders if it is equally effective at all stages of reading development in elementary school. Is it beneficial only when the child is in the early grades? Is it perhaps negatively related to achievement at higher stages of development, when children should be reading on their own?

Does going on field trips matter more to older children, who can understand and discuss the event at a deeper level, or does it mean more to younger children? Does watching television have a more positive effect on the reading achievement of young children, who are exposed through television to words they may not know? Does it perhaps have a negative effect on the reading development of older children, for whom the content and language of television are usually no longer a challenge?

Answers to such questions are important for several reasons. First, they can help confirm or disconfirm the validity of the developmental model of reading we used for the present study and thus deepen our understanding of how reading develops. In addition, they can lead to more specific suggestions to teachers and parents on the practices that lead to optimal development at various stages of reading development, ages, and grades. In this chapter we examine first the home factors (at grades 2, 4, and 6) and then the school factors (at grades 3, 5, and 7) that influence children's literacy development.

Home Conditions and Practices

For the younger children, various activities in the home involving adults were found to be strongly related to literacy development. Younger children who participated frequently in activities with adults, visited relatives frequently, and were part of extended families were more advanced in reading than those who participated in fewer such activities. These home activities were most strongly related to the literacy development of second graders; they were less strongly related to the literacy and language development of fourth graders, and not at all related to that of sixth graders. It appears that, for our population, and particularly for the younger children, literacy and language development benefited from many contacts with adults.

The provision of literacy in the home (for example, providing books and reading books to children) was also more highly related to the literacy development of the younger students (second and fourth graders) than to that of the older students (sixth graders). Thus, for our population of low-income children, the provision of a literacy environment proved to be more effective for the students in the earlier grades.

The literacy development of the older students was related more strongly to other home factors. Parental expectations and aspirations for their children's educational achievement predicted reading achievement for sixth graders but not for second and fourth graders. Both the level of family organization and its emotional stability were predictors of reading achievement among fourth and sixth graders, but not for second graders. In addition, a higher level of education and literacy of the mother was related to sixth graders' reading and vocabulary development—more than it was to the reading and vocabulary development of second graders.

Thus, we found that certain aspects of the home environment were more important for early literacy development while others were more important for later development. In a real sense, these findings could have been predicted from our developmental model of reading. To succeed at second grade reading, children need to learn what is taught to them in school; this learning is easier if children are supported by sufficient contact with adults and by greater provision for literacy in the home (for example, reading to the child and buying books). These home factors enhance children's language and their recognition of words (tasks important for primary grade reading). To succeed in sixth grade reading, on the other hand, children need to acquire larger vocabularies (particularly of less common, more difficult words); they need to read texts with new ideas and unfamiliar words and concepts, and they need to think about what they read. Thus, both highly literate and less literate parents might be equally effective with the child who is in the primary grades. However, more literate parents might be able to give more assistance to the child in the higher grades who needs to read more difficult texts.

One can also appreciate the value of stronger family organization and emotional stability for the literacy of older students. Literacy tasks in sixth grade require more concentration over longer periods of time than do such tasks in the second grade. The mother's more advanced literacy, her greater interest in reading, and her expression of high aspirations for her child's educational achievement seem to be more important in the later years of elementary school than in the earlier years.

Finally, our findings on the effects of frequent television viewing were not consistent. That television viewing affects reading differently depending on the age and grade of students has been reported by other researchers (Hornik, 1978, 1981). We did find more consistent evidence that heavier television viewing was associated with lower reading scores. For example, a significantly higher percentage of below-average readers (about 75 percent) watched television in the morning before school than did above-average readers (about 45 percent). Below-average readers were also twice as likely to watch television for more than four hours per day.

School Influences

As with the home factors, certain school practices were more highly correlated with the children's literacy development in the earlier than in the later grades, while others had the opposite effect. For children in grade 3, classrooms that practiced a single-skills emphasis produced positive effects. Another strong influence on the reading development of third graders was the use of challenging reading texts that were at the child's level of difficulty or above, but not below. The use of materials to supplement the basal reading texts also produced positive effects on third graders' reading. Thus, concentrated, challenging instruction from basal readers supplemented with other materials produced higher literacy among third graders.

For fifth graders, the classroom activities most highly associated with reading achievement were explicit comprehension instruction and the relation of reading instruction to the subject areas; such activity is typically recommended for children in the intermediate grades. (See Stage 3, reading for learning the new, in Table 1-2.)

Even more school factors were related to the seventh graders' reading. At this stage reading is a complex task requiring interrelated skills and abilities. Thus, as would be expected, a single-skills emphasis was negatively correlated to seventh grade reading achievement. Positive influences included teaching comprehension, using inference questioning, relating reading to subject areas, encouraging wide reading of a variety of materials, and providing library visits. All of these activities are recommended for this grade and stage of development (see Table 1-2).

Generally, the classroom practices that were positively correlated with the reading gains of children in grades 3, 5, and 7 were the practices considered appropriate for the stage of reading development typical for that grade. They are also the practices recommended in most textbooks for teachers on methods of teaching reading.

Home and School Practices: Examples

Examining the differences in influences on literacy by grade is helpful in understanding why some home and school factors, although beneficial for one age group, may not be for another. Good practices for second graders may not be good practices for fourth or for sixth graders. Similarly, instructional practices that may help the average readers in one class may not help those reading a grade or two above or below the average. At home, children may own many books, but if these books do not challenge the reader—if they are too much below their reading level—they may not affect reading development positively. There were some children in our population who benefited from numerous contacts with many adults; such contacts were associated positively with literacy in the early grades. Also associated positively with reading development in the early grades was reading to children, but this activity lost its influence in the higher grades.

Thus, some homes may provide more benefits for literacy development for younger than for older children. Similarly, many classrooms we observed provided literacy activities that were more optimally stimulating and challenging for older children than for younger, and vice versa. For example, in one teacher's reading lesson for sixth graders of average reading ability (that is, those reading close to grade level), the reading instruction seemed to be more suitable for a lower grade. The class read from a fairly easy sixth grade basal reader, and the teacher asked mainly literal comprehension questions that seemed well within the students' abilities to answer. The vocabulary practice also involved words that seemed to be within the knowledge of most of the students (for instance, *patience, wharf, factual, tub, building,* and *ideas*). At least for the middle and higher-level readers in this classroom, more challenging reading material and vocabulary lessons with more difficult words would have been more productive, as would have opportunities to discuss the texts and make inferences. By pitching the level of instruction below that of most of her students, this teacher may have been limiting the opportunities for literacy development.

A fourth grade teacher who created a warm and friendly atmosphere in her classroom presented a similarly unchallenging curriculum for the children in the class. The teacher organized many games, which the children enjoyed, and she provided cookies and rewards for winning the games. But, in general, the reading lessons were at levels that were well below most of the children's abilities. Class time was often devoted to checking children's answers to questions on worksheets they had completed on their own; and time was spent coloring pictures, an activity most would consider inappropriate for end-of-the-year fourth graders. Daily "sharing time" discussions provided useful opportunities for children to report their own experiences; however, the teacher did not try to stretch the children's language and thinking by introducing relevant, less familiar vocabulary, relating the children's reports to information of a less personal nature, or asking questions about the reports that would challenge them to make connections to history, geography, science, or other subject areas.

Classrooms, like homes, can enhance the literacy and language development of children by providing experiences and practice at an appropriate stage of development. Many of the classrooms we observed lacked challenge and materials that would help enhance development—in the later grades as well as the earlier.

Conclusions

The differences we found in both home and school effects on literacy achievement among the children in the earlier and later grades bring us back to the model on which this study is based: reading goes through qualitative changes as it develops. Because the reading task goes through qualitative changes at different stages of development, we would expect that the home and school factors that facilitate reading development would differ by stage as well, and this is indeed what we found. Homes that are associated with higher reading scores in the early grades provide a good literacy environment (reading to the child, buying books) and time with other adults. Older children benefit most from homes that have high expectations for their educational attainment and stimulate their child to learn.

In school, children in the lower grades benefit from an emphasis on structure and challenging texts (that is, on or slightly above their reading levels) as well as from the use of reading materials other than a reading textbook. In the higher grades (fourth through seventh grades), when reading becomes more complex, classrooms that have a positive effect on reading achievement and vocabulary expose the students to a variety of activities to develop comprehension, using different genres and content of considerable complexity and challenge. Direct instruction and questioning in comprehension are also helpful in these middle grades.

The nature of the reading task changes as children grow older, becoming increasingly complex. For our population, both family and school played critical roles in promoting reading development. In the higher grades, however, our data suggest that the school plays the larger role.

10

Where Do We Go from Here?

What have we learned about the development of reading, writing, and language among low-income children? When and why do they run into difficulties? What can be done to overcome and prevent these difficulties?

Our most significant finding is that the low-income children in our population achieved well in reading, as well as the general population, up through the third grade. Then, beginning around grade 4, their reading achievement began to slump; the slump intensified through grade 7 and continued through high school. Equally important, if not more so, is our finding that certain school and home conditions lead to higher than expected literacy achievement and that these conditions, if implemented, can alleviate the downward trends in literacy that begin around grade 4.

The purpose of this chapter is to present the main conclusions of our study, together with recommendations arising from it for educational practitioners and policymakers. We hope as well that researchers will see questions that need further confirmation, clarification, and challenge. Overall, although we recognize the limitations of our study—the small sample of children, the fact that our population may be less "disadvantaged" than others of low-income status, the fact that the schools and teachers were perhaps better than most others who teach low-income children—we are confident that what we found and what we recommend can improve the situation. Indeed, most of our findings are continuous with past research and with theory on language and literacy development. Our recommendations focus on what the teacher, the school administrator, the teacher trainer, and the book publisher can do to prevent the deceleration in literacy—procedures that, to a great extent, have been and continue to be used to bring excellence in literary achievement to all children.

Conclusions

Reading

The most significant finding for reading in our study was the strong achievement among our low-income children in grades 2 and 3. In these early grades they achieved on a par with national norms—that is, as well as children in the general population—on all reading tests as well as on their knowledge of word meanings. At this point, differences between the students designated as above-average and below-average readers were small.

It did not come as a surprise that the low-income children in our sample had no particular difficulties with the early stages of reading. The main task of reading in the primary grades is to learn the alphabetic principle—to recognize words, to decode, and to read familiar texts (see Table 1-2; see also Chall, 1983b, 1989b; Adams, 1989). These children knew the meanings of words that others in their grades knew. Their main task was to learn to recognize words, decode, and read fluently; the schools and teachers provided the instruction they needed, and the children benefited from it (see Chapter 7).

As predicted by the theoretical model of reading used for our study (see Chapter 1), the students' scores started to slump at about grade 4. For the below-average readers, the slump began early (in grade 4) and was intense. By grades 6 and 7, they were reading almost two years below grade level on all the reading tests. For the above-average readers, the slump began later (around grade 6) and was less intense. Many of the above-average readers were still reading on grade level or above in the sixth and seventh grades on some of the reading tests.

The slump started earlier on some tests than on others. The first to slip was vocabulary. Although the entire group, both good and poor readers, did as well as the general population in defining words in grades 2 and 3 (common, high-frequency words), they began to have difficulty defining the more abstract, academic, literary, and uncommon words tested in grades 4 through 7. By grade 7 they were more than two years below norms on word meanings; thus they did not know the less common, academic, and abstract words needed for reading their texts in science and social studies, as well as their library books, newspapers, and magazines. Next to decelerate were their scores on word recognition and spelling. Oral reading and silent reading comprehension scores decelerated last.

Overall, the students seemed to have less difficulty with tasks that supplied context (oral and silent reading) and more difficulty with tasks that did not supply context (word meaning, word recognition, spelling). Put another way, they scored better on tests of "reading for meaning" than on tests of skills that underlie meaningful reading—meanings of words, accurate word recognition, and spelling of longer and less common words. Thus, on the whole, their relative strengths in grades 4 to 7 lay in the cognitive and contextual aspects of reading, and their relative weakness was on tasks requiring greater precision with individual words, tested out of context (that is, giving the definitions of less common and more abstract words, and identifying and spelling accurately more difficult words). This finding seems to run counter to many current theories of reading, which suggest that low scores on reading tests come primarily from weaknesses in reading comprehension, particularly with higher-level cognitive processing, rather than from underlying difficulties with word recognition and word meaning (see Anderson et al., 1985; Applebee, Langer, and Mullis, 1987).

Starting in grade 4, the above-average and below-average readers began to pull apart. The below-average readers slumped earlier and more intensely; for the above-average group, the slump came later and was milder. The difference in fluency was considerable: all of the above-average readers in grades 2 through 7 were fluent readers, while most of the below-average readers were dysfluent.

Thus, if we view reading as composed of three basic components—cognition, language, and reading skills (Carroll, 1977)—cognition did not seem to be the major problem for our population. They did best from grades 4 to 7 on the tests that required them to get meaning from and put meaning into what they read—reading comprehension and connected oral reading. (It should be recalled that in grades 2 and 3 they did equally well on all the tests.) Their worst performance was on the tests that can be classified as being close to "basic" for reading—defining less familiar words presented orally and out of context, and identifying less common, single words and spelling them, also out of context. These basic measures have traditionally been considered to be teachable, and have traditionally been seen as the responsibility of the school. Further, the vast research and theory on reading indicate that these basics are essential for the development of reading comprehension (see Chall, 1989b).

Writing

The findings on writing are essentially similar to those for reading. In our sample, greater gains were made on writing in the early grades than in the later grades. On most measures, the gains were greater from grade 2 to grade 4, and relatively smaller from grade 4 to grade 7. The patterns of writing for the below-average and above-average readers were also similar to those for reading; deceleration in writing started earlier and was stronger for the below-average readers as compared to the above-average group, especially on exposition.

A third similarity between reading and writing concerns the students' relative strengths and weaknesses on the different components of writing. Generally, most of the children scored better on the writing measures concerned with the maturity and quality of the content (that is, ideas) as compared to the form (use of grammar, punctuation, spelling, and sentence structure). The students had ideas to express but lacked precise form with which to express those ideas. A final similarity to reading was the students' use of only the most common words. Only rarely did any of the students use uncommon words, even in grade 7. Thus, in writing as in reading, the students performed better on "meaning-making" tasks (that is, higher in content than in form).

Language

The findings from the language measures also tend to confirm those from reading and writing. The two additional vocabulary tests included in the language measures—one a test of familiarity with words and the other a measure of precision and sophistication in defining words—confirmed the findings from the word meaning test in the reading battery. The students did well in grades 2 and 3, but began to slump at about grade 4. The familiarity scores were higher than the scores for precision and sophistication in vocabulary. In other aspects of language, however, the children in our study seemed to develop at a normal rate. They did well on tests of grammar and language awareness, and there were minimal differences between the above-average and below-average readers. Thus, on most of the language tests, the trends were less consistent than for the reading and writing tests. In general, the grammar and language awareness scores were less highly related to reading achievement than were the vocabulary measures.

Overall, our population seemed to have basic language abilities, and they demonstrated mastery starting early and continuing through the third grade. What they seemed to lack most, starting around grade 4, was knowledge of less common, more academic words; words beyond the elemental; words that are learned in school; and words required to read and understand the books used in the intermediate and upper elementary grades. This lack of knowledge and skill with words beyond the most common in the English language was also found to hinder their writing development.

In sum, at all grades—2 through 7—our low-income population seemed to have the basic linguistic competencies (as shown in their grammar and language awareness test scores and in their word meaning knowledge through grade 3) and cognitive competencies (as shown on their stronger scores on oral and silent reading comprehension than on measures that tested "the basics"). Why, then, was there an increasing slump in their reading and writing achievement, beginning around the fourth grade?

One hypothesis is that their reading skills and knowledge of word meanings, which were sufficient for reading through grade 3, were not sufficient for grades 4 and beyond, when students are expected to read more complex materials (see Chapter 1). While reading at grade 4 and beyond requires students to be fluent in word recognition and decoding, it also requires that they know the meanings of words that are less common, more abstract, and more literary—that is, words that are acquired through formal education. Another reason for the difficulty these students experienced in making the transition to harder texts in grades 4 and beyond may stem from a lack of fluency, particularly among the below-average readers. Those who lacked fluency read slowly and hesitatingly—conditions that tend to result ultimately in less reading on the part of the student and greater difficulty with silent reading comprehension.

What were the school and home conditions that influenced literacy and language achievement? Did any seem to alleviate or prevent the fourth-grade slump?

Home and School Influences

The conditions in the children's homes that were positively related to reading achievement in grades 2 and 3 were adult interaction with children and homes that provided a good literacy environment. Happily, we found that most homes provided these. However, the home conditions that facilitated reading achievement in grades 4 to 7, which included higher educational and literacy attainment of the parents and parental interest in the educational achievement of their children, were not as common. These conditions, which we found to be positively associated with literacy development in grades 4 to 7, are not as easily modified as the conditions that are associated with early literacy development. Thus, the school's role assumes greater importance for the literacy development of low-income children in grades 4 to 7.

What school factors helped the children make a good transition in literacy and language from the primary to the intermediate grades? First, the children in our sample had a strong reading program in the early grades, which, according to school reports, included the use of a widely used basal reading series, supplemented by a separate phonics program and the reading of library books. This program was effective for most of these children; at the end of grades 2 and 3, they achieved on grade norms.

Different school conditions affected different aspects of literacy and language development in the primary and the intermediate grades. (See Chandler and Hemphill, 1983, for the findings reported here.) For the whole population, structure (difficulty level of reading text and workbook homework) and challenge (difficulty of instructional materials on or above the reading level of the student, not below) had a positive influence on all aspects of reading—on word recognition, comprehension, and word meanings. The teaching of higher-level processes and enrichment were particularly effective for the development of vocabulary (word meaning) and reading comprehension, but not for word recognition. Vocabulary development also benefited from structure and challenge and from the availability and use of a wide variety of materials in addition to textbooks. Reading comprehension improved with the use of challenging materials and with direct instruction and practice using these more difficult materials.

Some school influences were more effective in certain grades and less effective in others. Structure and challenge had a strong positive influence in both the primary and the intermediate grades; use of a variety of materials and direct teaching of comprehension and word meanings were more effective in the intermediate grades. Higher-level instruction that focuses on making inferences and reacting critically to what is read had strong positive effects on reading comprehension especially in the later grades; it was weak or had negative effects in the early grades, especially on the development of word recognition. Enrichment (that is, the use of many books besides textbooks) had a positive effect on vocabulary gains, substantial positive effects on reading comprehension, but no effect on word recognition.

Thus, there appeared to be no one set of best practices for teaching reading that applied to all grades and all aspects of reading. As would be predicted by the stages of reading development, the effectiveness of various practices depended on the level of development of the children. In the lower grades, when the students needed work in word recognition, the most effective conditions were structure (the use of basal readers and workbooks) and appropriate challenge. Emphasis on enrichment and higher-level processes was not as effective in the lower grades; indeed, it had negative results on word recognition. For the children who had made the transition to an intermediate level, focus on higher-level processes and enrichment was more productive; it was associated with greater development of word meanings, one of the major needs in the middle grades.

Recommendations

Do Low-Income Children Need Different Reading Programs?

Our major recommendation, based on our findings and the best knowledge to date, is that the literacy instruction given to low-income children be essentially the same as that used successfully with most children. We differ, then, from many others whose theories and proposed solutions have focused on the differences in these children and on the use of different methods and materials to overcome their literacy lags.

We offer this recommendation for the following reasons. First, these children had strengths in language and reading in the early grades that were on a par with those of mainstream children. Second, they thrived on the regular reading program to which they were exposed during grades 2 and 3, a program that is also effective with mainstream children; as a group, our students scored on grade level on all the reading tests administered. Third, the course of development of these children on the various components of reading, writing, and language was similar to that found among other children—in the primary grades. Some components began to slump in the middle grades as compared to the performance of mainstream children. But these slumps can be understood when particular conditions in the home and school are taken into account. What is even more important, these lags can be overcome and prevented when more positive conditions are provided, particularly by the school.

Thus we believe that if adjustments in the instructional program are made, particularly as the children approach fourth grade, the typical slumps found in their reading achievement can be prevented. Indeed, most effective reading programs incorporate adjustments to the needs of different children—to the needs of the gifted, to higher achievers, to average students, and to English as a Second Language students.

Perhaps the strongest reason for not having a separate reading program for low-income children is that different programs tend to separate children from others not like themselves. For broad educational, social, and civic reasons, being part of a larger community is more beneficial for low-income children and for society. Moreover, if their instruction proceeds at a slower pace because they are in a different program, it will be even more difficult for them to catch up.

Overall, we recommend as a guide the instruction proposed as optimal for most children (see Chall, 1983b; Anderson et al., 1985). These guides, based on a synthesis of research, suggest the early teaching of word recognition skills; systematic, explicit phonics; and connected reading, with the use of both basal readers and trade books (story and informational books) for the primary grades. The use of enriched, literature-based beginning reading programs, a recent trend, may be less effective unless such programs are combined with the structure and appropriate challenge provided by most textbooks (see Chapter 7).

The need of low-income children in grade 4 to learn more uncommon, "academic" words is shared by middle-class children in this grade. Indeed, an essential aspect of most reading curricula, as well as the curricula in specific subject areas for the intermediate and upper elementary grades, is the development of word meanings. Our low-income children's need for greater vocabulary knowledge is thus similar to that of middle-class children. It is not a difference in kind, only a difference in amount.

Thus, the needs of low-income children are not really special needs; they are the same needs as for most children. Because the low-income child's family may not provide as much stimulation in language and literacy, the school must take on more of this responsibility. But this is not a new responsibility for the schools, for they have always been responsible for the teaching of language and literacy.

Development of the Fourth-Grade Slump

The schools should become more sensitive to the course of development of reading and language among low-income children as they advance through the grades, particularly beginning around the fourth grade. This awareness, important for all children, is critical for low-income children; for the earlier they start to slip, the faster they fall, and the farther behind they are in each succeeding grade (see Stanovich, 1986). Literacy and language develop over many years; if students fall behind, they seldom right themselves without special help. Instead, the momentum of the decline intensifies. Thus, it is important for policy planners, schools, and families to assess the reading difficulties of these children as early as possible and to help them overcome their weaknesses. It is even more important to design programs that anticipate the particular needs of low-income children. Because of the developmental nature of reading, the later one waits, the more difficult it is for the children to cope with the increasing demands of reading in the later grades. Moreover, those who have reading difficulties in the intermediate grades will have serious trouble not only with their reading lessons but with the study of science, social studies, literature, mathematics, and other subjects that are learned, in part, from printed text.

If children are weak in one reading skill, other components and the total act of reading will be affected. For example, if word recognition is weak, fluency will be affected negatively, as will silent reading comprehension. Inaccuracy and lack of fluency tend also to lower the students' motivation to read for pleasure; as a result, overall reading achievement will suffer because the more outside reading a student does, the higher the reading achievement. A limited meaning vocabulary also has a negative effect on both fluency and rate of reading and the ability to comprehend difficult texts. Thus, it is important that low-income children receive early attention when they begin to fall behind and that they be assessed and given instruction appropriate to their difficulties and their strengths.

Overall, the low-income children in our sample were strongest in reading comprehension and in other cognitive and linguistic aspects of reading. They had little difficulty understanding connected texts, using basic grammar and language, and understanding the meanings of the common words in the language. They did have difficulty, however, with defining less familiar, longer, and more specialized words, and with identifying such words in print and spelling them.

Why should low-income children have greater difficulty than middle-class children with the meanings of less familiar words? It would seem that middle-class children have a double chance of learning more advanced ideas and words because they have more highly educated parents, who read to them more, and because middle-class children also read more themselves (they own more books).

Policy Decisions for the Reading Curriculum

Policy issues concerning the reading curriculum are the responsibility of many—of researchers and scholars; those who train teachers; superintendents; school principals; directors of reading and language arts; classroom teachers; and, in some communities, parent groups. They decide what to teach and when to teach it, as well as what to stress in which grades. Also responsible for these decisions are the authors and publishers of textbooks and other educational materials, particularly those who publish the basal reading programs used by more than 95 percent of all children in the early grades. Thus, improvement in practices is the responsibility of many people, not just the teachers; what teachers do is often based on a general consensus that is incorporated in methods texts on the teaching of reading, instructional materials, and guidebooks for teachers produced by educational publishers.

What program emphasis is best for low-income children? Should there be stress on basic skills, particularly on word recognition and phonics; on comprehension and language; or on a more open use of literature and writing? Our findings suggest different emphases for different aspects of reading. Vocabulary gains were associated with the use of challenging reading texts; comprehension gains were associated with allocated time for reading and explicit comprehension instruction. Both were associated with the use of a variety of materials. We also found that reliance on one style or emphasis does not promote all aspects of reading. Word recognition and reading comprehension for our low-income children were developed best when the teacher used structural materials such as basal readers and workbooks and assigned homework from these. Vocabulary gains (word meanings) were greater in classrooms that had rich literacy environments containing a wide variety of materials. However, classrooms that focused solely on varied materials sacrificed gains in word recognition.

We do not recommend, therefore, a reading program that follows an extreme—one that focuses only on a more highly structured reading system, with little time for reading, or one that uses only trade books, dropping explicit teaching of skills. Our study also proposes caution in the exclusive use of one focus or the other. In grades 4 to 7, we found that the exclusive use of basal readers, with direct teaching of comprehension strategies, was associated with better than expected gains in word recognition and comprehension. On the other hand, an enriched reading program with almost exclusive use of a wide variety of trade books was associated with higher scores in vocabulary meanings.

For the primary grades, a reading program that was goal-directed, structured, and challenging but also provided for wide reading of trade books produced good results. Such programs focused on teaching recognition and decoding skills as well as on practice in reading stories with understanding. In addition to basal readers, they made use of a variety of literature, which helped give practice in fluent reading and exposed the children to challenging words and ideas.

In the following paragraphs we discuss several of the broad characteristics observed in classrooms that led to either gains or losses in various aspects of reading.

Hard or Easy? A strong factor influencing the reading achievement of low-income children in the primary and intermediate grades is the level of difficulty of the materials used for instruction. This was found both in the present study and in many previous studies (Chall and Feldmann, 1966; Chall, Conard, and Harris, 1977; Chall et al., 1983). Generally, we recommend that for instruction directed and guided by the teacher, the level of difficulty be challenging—neither too easy nor too hard. In our study, a level either on or somewhat above the students' reading level was more effective than a level below the students' reading achievement. A challenging level was associated with good gains in all aspects of reading—word recognition, comprehension, and word meanings.

This recommendation may seem to some to run counter to general practice, since for more than five decades teachers and reading specialists have preferred an easy rather than a challenging match of students and instructional materials, particularly for low-income students (Conard, 1981). Our findings and recommendations for challenging materials confirm Vygotsky's theory (1962) of the zone of proximal development—that when instruction is provided, learning is optimal when it precedes, rather than follows, the child's level of development. What we recommend, therefore, is that instruction be on a level from which children can learn with the aid of a teacher or more knowledgeable peers—a level usually above their present achievement (Chall et al., 1983).

The Importance of Fluency. Fluency and automaticity (that is, the quick recognition of words and phrases) are critical underlying factors for effective reading, particularly in grade 2 and beyond. (See Chapter 1, Reading Stages.) Wide reading is essential to the development of automaticity and fluency. Therefore, collections of literature and information books of high quality need to be made available in the classroom, particularly for low-SES children, who have fewer books at home than middle-class children. Time needs to be set aside in the classroom for the use of such books, and the children should be encouraged to take the books home for reading. In addition, teachers should try other ways of developing fluency, such as simultaneous reading of books while listening to tapes (Chomsky, 1978), using traditional flash cards, and having students take turns reading aloud with the teacher or more advanced peers as models (Chall and Curtis, 1987). Accurate word recognition and decoding in the early grades and wide practice of these skills in the reading of connected texts are also essential in developing fluency, particularly in the primary grades.

The Special Case of Vocabulary in the Middle Grades. From fourth grade on, our population of low-income students did poorly on vocabulary or word meanings. Their performance was consistently poor on the two vocabulary measures of the language battery, on the word meaning test in the reading battery, and on the writing samples (on which they seldom used uncommon words). In grades 2 and 3 they had scored on grade level in vocabulary when the words tested were words of high frequency in the English language. But in fourth grade and beyond, when they were asked to define abstract, literary, and technical words that are usually acquired in school, they tested considerably below grade level.

Our findings suggest the need for a serious look at how to accelerate the rate of vocabulary acquisition, particularly of the less common, literary, abstract words needed for reading, writing, and understanding in grade 4 and beyond. Two questions need to be considered: When should we start teaching vocabulary? And what method and materials would be most effective?

With regard to the timing, the research evidence offers some guidelines. Six-year-olds have listening and speaking vocabularies of about 6,000 words; thus the major focus in a primary-grade reading program might best be placed on accurate word recognition, decoding, and fluent reading. It is unclear whether the trend during the 1980s of teaching word meanings (and multiple meanings of words) in the primary-level basal readers has fulfilled its promise (Meyer, 1989). Perhaps the best explanation for this is that the word meanings taught may have been words the children already knew. There is no question, however, that, beginning at about grade 3 or 4, these children need a systematic emphasis on the development of word meanings.

But vocabulary acquisition can be accelerated in the primary grades by several approaches. One is by reading and also by being read to. But reading to children in the primary grades may not be as effective as expected if the books read to them are already within their reading ability and if the time spent listening to books is taken from the time they should spend reading books. Thus, to be effective, the books read to the children should be challenging; that is, they should contain vocabulary and syntax beyond what is used for instruction in reading. In addition, it should be noted that being read to cannot be a substitute for reading practice (see Meyer, 1989). Our study also found that the reading textbooks used for instruction are more effective when they are on a level that challenges the student, not on a level below the student's achievement. Another way to develop interest in word meanings among young children in the primary grades is playing and having fun with words—finding word origins and inventing words.

More is known about how to teach vocabulary in the fourth grade and beyond. The research has been growing on the effectiveness of various methods of teaching vocabulary, and many of them have been found effective. These methods can be divided roughly into those that stress direct instruction and those that rely on acquiring vocabulary from wide reading of increasingly difficult texts. In the present study, challenge and a rich literacy environment were found to be effective for developing word meaning (as well as reading comprehension). Wide reading exposed these low-income children to new words. Other studies have found that the direct teaching of word meanings also produces effective results. For specific methods of teaching vocabulary, see Dale and O'Rourke (1971), Johnson and Pearson (1984), Graves (1987), and Nagy (1989).

Should Reading Textbooks Be Used? Until quite recently, textbooks for teaching reading—basal readers, workbooks, and teacher's manuals—were the materials used almost universally in the elementary schools. During the past few years, various groups, who call their view "whole language," have proposed that basal readers be abandoned for "real literature," without the teaching of skills, and through the combining of reading and writing. It is difficult to know how many classrooms have moved to a whole-language approach and particularly how many schools with high concentrations of low-income children have done this. There are few research data offered on the effectiveness of the whole-language approach. A recent analysis by Stahl and Miller (1989) of studies that compared whole-language and basal-reader approaches found that only in kindergarten did the children seem to benefit more from the whole-language approach. In first grade, although both approaches tended to produce similar effects, children in those programs that had stronger instruction in phonics tended to score higher. The conclusion was that it was important in kindergarten to concentrate on functions of written language, while in first grade it was important to concentrate on the connection between letters and sounds in spoken words. (See Chall's Reading Stages, Stages 0 and 1, Table 1-2.)

Our study offers evidence that both reading textbooks and wider reading beyond them lead to positive results. The use of reading textbooks (basal readers) and workbooks was associated in our study with more than expected gains in word recognition and comprehension (see Chapter 7). But the exclusive use of basal readers and workbooks was not enough—particularly for grade 4 and beyond. The children in our sample who were in classrooms that used trade books, encyclopedias, and other reference books (in addition to basal reading textbooks) and who spent time reading their subject-matter textbooks made greater gains than expected. Exposure to books on a variety of subjects and on a wide range of difficulty levels was particularly effective in the development of vocabulary and reading comprehension.

Wide reading was especially important for building the vocabularies of our low-income children, beginning at about grade 4. Visits to libraries were also related to better reading achievement. Thus it seems clear that, to improve the reading and language development of low-income children, they must read more widely. To facilitate this, books must be made accessible to them in the classroom, in the school library, and in the public library (for the importance of availability of books, see Marston, 1982).

Writing

Our findings strongly support increased instruction and practice in writing starting in the primary grades. Little writing instruction occurred in the schools we observed. The children who were required to write selections of at least a paragraph in length were better writers; quasi-writing (such as filling in blanks, copying poems from the blackboard or definitions from dictionaries, and doing worksheets) did not enhance the children's writing skills. Further, the children who practiced writing longer passages showed greater gains in reading comprehension.

Clearly, the classrooms of low-income students need to devote more time to writing. What writing they did do in their classrooms was personal or narrative writing. Little practice was observed in expository writing.

Much has been written about the advantages and disadvantages of various methods of teaching writing to low-income children. Our findings indicate that they need practice not only in the process or meaning-making aspects of writing, but also in the precise aspects of form in which they were particularly weak: syntax, mechanics, spelling, and punctuation. Further, they could profit from better and increased instruction in vocabulary, especially that vocabulary needed for reading and writing in grade 4 and beyond: words that are less common in everyday, conventional, spoken language and more characteristic of academic discourse. In our study, even the writing of the best readers in grade 4 and beyond used only the most concrete, frequently used words. The content of their writing, ultimately, was affected by the limited vocabulary with which they expressed themselves; it was also limited by their uncertain knowledge of form.

Relation of Literacy Instruction to Other Curricular Areas

The most difficult words children are likely to encounter, particularly in the middle elementary grades, are in their subject area textbooks. Yet the classrooms we observed made little use of opportunities during social studies or science instruction to teach vocabulary and to provide guidance in reading and studying those texts. In classes where the teachers did teach "content reading," the intermediate-grade children made better gains. Teaching reading and writing in the various curricular areas has been proposed for generations; it is especially needed by low-income children for vocabulary development.

Home/School Collaboration

Report Cards. The low-income families in our study had, in general, high aspirations and expectations for their children's educational achievement. However, their understanding of their children's progress often differed from that of the child's teacher. Many parents in our study had an incomplete or an incorrect idea about their children's status as readers and as learners; many parents thought their children were achieving much better than they actually were. The parents based their judgments of their children's progress on their grades, which were often inflated or were based on the child's aptitude. Often, parents were unaware of what a particular grade meant. Thus, many parents whose children received B's and C's felt their children were making adequate progress, and they rarely undertook special action to ensure better performance in the future. The teachers often interpreted lack of parental reaction as disinterest. As a result, many children slipped below grade level without the benefit of either parental or school-based intervention.

We recommend that schools use grading and reporting procedures that are consistent and that communicate to parents how well their child is doing. Perhaps two grades could be used—one based on achievement in relation to school-wide and nation-wide norms, and one reflecting achievement and progress in relation to the child's aptitudes.

Contacts with Parents. As expected, parental contact with schools was important for several reasons. During personal contacts, parents can express their interest and concern about their children's achievement, teachers can explain grades, and both parties can discuss problems before they become more serious. In our study, contacts between parents and teachers often resulted in a change in teachers' estimates of the helpfulness of the child's home. Generally, both teacher-initiated and parent-initiated contacts were helpful in improving children's progress. Yet many teachers and parents never met in the course of an entire year. The parents in our study tended to expect teachers to contact them if their children were experiencing academic difficulties; the teachers, at the same time, expected the parents to get in touch with them if their children received poor grades. Especially for the older children, there was considerable miscommunication: since almost all teacher-initiated contacts concerned discipline, parents rarely thought their children had academic problems; since parents rarely contacted teachers about academic issues, the teachers concluded that the parents had little interest in their children's academic achievement.

Schools need to address this cycle of miscommunication. Regular contact between the school and the home can only serve to improve parents' understanding of their children's progress.

Homework and Interacting with Adults. Our findings from the home observations and interviews indicate that children who spend time alone with adults have an advantage over children who spend most of their time with siblings and peers. This relation was particularly noticeable for the vocabulary and language measures. Such a finding is not surprising, since dialogue with an adult is likely to be more challenging linguistically and more informative about the world than dialogue with another child.

In middle-class homes, homework is often an opportunity for sharing between children and adults. For many low-income parents, however, who may not have the time to help their children or who may not be conversant with the lessons their children get in the middle and upper elementary grades, homework may not serve this function. We found that many of the children in our study were more likely to turn to older siblings than to parents for help with homework.

For younger children in the primary grades, a few innovative teachers in our study assigned homework especially designed to involve parents—for example, having the parents read aloud to the children or vice versa. Some teachers asked older children to interview adult family members about various topics and to discuss an article from the newspaper with an adult as preparation for a report on current events.

We recommend that the school be aware of the fact that, beginning with the middle and upper elementary grades, many parents of low-income children cannot provide the help with homework that may be needed. Thus, homework assignments particularly for the older children should be designed in such a way that children can complete them independently or that parents can understand the kind of help they are expected to provide.

Advice to Families

Provision of Literacy

The provision of literacy to children by their parents promotes the children's acquisition of reading skill.* In the earlier grades, reading to children, encouraging them to read aloud, and taking them to libraries are all important. Not just reading, but also *re*reading books is important for developing children's reading. Thus, children should visit libraries and own some favorite books. Furthermore, if the televi-

*We present here only those recommendations for parents that relate to home-school collaboration; see Snow et al. (forthcoming) for other recommendations.

sion is turned off for some hours each day, children may be likely to read more often.

Time with Adults

We found that spending time with adults, especially adults who engaged in a variety of activities, was related to low-income children's literacy skill development. Thus, the time that children spend with their parents as well as with adult extended family members, neighbors, and friends is a valuable resource. Society provides many opportunities for children to interact with adults, including adult-supervised after-school centers, story hours in libraries, big brother/sister programs, school or community-based vacation activities, and lessons and programs organized in community centers. The growth in language and literacy that children can experience in these situations can easily justify the salaries of the adults and teenagers needed to run such programs (Baldwin, 1986).

Contact with the School

Parents should visit their children's teachers. The teachers in our study were more likely to have higher expectations for children whose parents they had met. During visits with teachers, parents can ask teachers about their children's grades; make sure their children are doing as well as they can in terms of class, school, and nationwide norms; and explore with the teacher how to help their children. Teachers, in turn, have a chance during such meetings to discuss problems as they arise. Schools should make parents feel welcome in their children's classrooms and encourage them to visit at regular intervals. Parents should find opportunities to meet with principals and special teachers as well. School-home relations are a two-way street: although the schools must provide avenues for communication, parents must take advantage of them.

When a Child Begins to Slip

Our results, and those of other studies, suggest that once a child falls behind in reading, writing, or language, deceleration is likely to increase with each succeeding grade. Thus, when children begin to slip, they need immediate, special instruction. Parents should consult the teacher as soon as the child begins to slip; they should request an assessment and extra help if it is indicated. If a student is below average in reading in the intermediate grades, parents can assist in subject-area study by reading the texts aloud to the child. It is critical that parents be aware of their child's progress and that they act in partnership with the school to ensure the child's best development. If the school cannot provide the diagnostic and remedial services needed, parents should seek out other resources, such as a reading laboratory or clinic in a university or hospital. What is essential is that the child not be left to slip farther and farther behind.

Overcoming Obstacles to Improvement

Our recommendations for preventing the fourth-grade slump in the literacy development of low-income children are, for the most part, not dramatically different from recommendations made for the literacy development of most children. Various aspects of our recommendations can be found in the literature going back to at least the 1920s. The importance of direct teaching of reading and word meanings using challenging materials as well as the importance of wide reading for acquiring reading skills and for developing lifetime habits in reading was stressed by early investigators (see Terman and Lima, 1926). Moreover, much of what we found has long been known intuitively by teachers and administrators. Why, then, one may ask, has the literacy level of low-income children remained low when general knowledge for improving literacy has long been available? There are many explanations; here we discuss only a few. We present these explanations not as excuses, but in recognition that many obstacles need to be overcome if we are to improve the literacy of children-at-risk as well as of those in the mainstream.

Perhaps the greatest obstacle is that schools have not been able to provide state-of-the-art programs and instruction for either mainstream or at-risk children. Although mainstream students perform better than low-income and minority students, even they do not reach a level of literacy achievement that is appropriate for their cognitive abilities. According to the National Assessment of Educational Progress, only 39 percent of U.S. high school seniors were able to read, with understanding, textbooks appropriate for their grade. Their achievement in writing, mathematics, science, and history was equally low (Chall, Conard, and Harris, 1977; NAEP, 1989). Why have the schools had such problems in developing literacy among students and particularly among low-income children?

We turn first to the training of teachers, because they are, in the final analysis, the ones who provide the literacy environment and the instruction that make the difference between learning well and not learning well. They decide on appropriate levels of instruction and on assignments, and they must blow the whistle when students' achievement lags behind their cognitive abilities. They must collaborate with other professionals—reading specialists, psychologists, speech and language specialists, social workers, neurologists—when a child needs special help. To do these things well, particularly with at-risk children, requires more than the preservice training in the teaching of reading that most teachers receive. Few teachers have sufficient theoretical knowledge and practical skills to teach reading to at-risk children successfully. Knowledge about literacy, its development, and its teaching changes; thus schools must provide for teachers' continued professional growth. Yet funds for such activities are sorely limited, and they are particularly limited for the teachers who teach low-income children.

Another reason for the less than optimal state of literacy programs in schools is the uncertainty and confusion surrounding such concepts as the appropriate level of difficulty for instruction, the effective use of content materials, and whether literacy instruction should have the same or a different focus in the primary and the later grades.

The issue of optimal difficulty of instruction for achievement is an old one. Increasingly, the research evidence of the past decade points to the importance of high expectations on the part of teachers and the use of challenging materials for optimal instruction and learning. This runs counter to the research and recommendations of the past 50 years, which tended to favor textbooks and instruction well within student achievement in order to "make them feel successful" and "not to frustrate them." In a recent study, teachers said they approved of challenging materials for high-achieving students but not for low achievers (Conard, 1981). Teachers are influenced by the publishers, who must also deal with this question. Generally, publishers try to produce textbooks that will be suitable for most students in a given grade. Yet relatively few of the available subject-matter textbooks are on a level that is appropriate for the lower achievers.

The place of subject-area textbooks in the teaching of reading is still uncertain, although the importance of connecting the two has been recognized at least since the 1920s. Everyone agrees that reading and writing belong "across the curriculum." Yet observations of fourth and eighth grade classrooms reveal that little time is spent on reading of subject-area materials, particularly in science and social studies. Moreover, little time is devoted to teaching the special vocabularies in these subjects or strategies for comprehending the information from text. Most instructional time is spent teaching from reading texts and trade books that are mainly fiction and are less challenging than the content textbooks (Harris-Sharples, 1983).

Why, when theory and research over many decades have recommended the use of expository, subject-matter texts and materials for teaching reading in the intermediate grades, has so little been done in this area? Some have suggested that the answer lies in the popular movement to make content more meaningful through "hands-on experiences" rather than the reading of texts. Thus, science is taught mainly through experiments and social studies, through "relevant" discussions. Textbooks, as a source of information, have been considered less important. As a result, children often do not learn how to read from texts—how to remember what they read, how to make generalizations and inferences, and how to write about what they have learned.

For teachers of low-achieving students, the hands-on approach may not be so much an instructional preference as a major means of survival. Because such students may be several years below grade level in reading by the seventh and eighth grades, and since almost all of the published textbooks on appropriate topics for these grades are designed for "average" readers, they find their textbooks too challenging—that is, too much beyond their reading abilities. Unfortunately, publishers have not produced the kinds of subject-matter materials that are optimally challenging for the lower one-quarter to one-third of students—those who are at risk. Thus, for low-income students, not being exposed to reading science and social studies limits what they can learn in these subjects; it also limits their reading practice and their achievement in the higher-level skills and promotes the deceleration of their literacy and language development.

Another area in which practice lags behind theory is the provision of a variety of reading materials in classrooms (textbooks, trade books, reference works) covering a wide range of subjects and difficulty. No one will debate the idea that a rich literacy environment is helpful for achievement in literacy. Yet if we were to survey a random sample of elementary school classrooms in the United States on any one day of the school year, we would find too many classrooms that do not have even enough textbooks for each child. Classrooms often lack a small library of story and informational books, and few classrooms have enough encyclopedias and dictionaries for all students. Moreover, the greater the number of at-risk children in the school, the more limited is the print environment in the classrooms and in the school.

Books cost money, and many schools say they cannot afford textbooks in the basic subjects for each child, let alone an encyclopedia, dictionaries, and trade books for each classroom. Some schools have so few books that they cannot send them home with the children for homework. Yet sending books home is particularly important for low-income children, who do not have many books at home. Indeed, they have significantly fewer than do mainstream children (NAEP, 1985).

State-of-the-art reading programs have available diagnostic and remedial services for those students who need them, and as early as they need them. But few schools can actually provide these services for all the children who need them. Declining funds over the past 15 years have resulted in decreased rather than increased services. Low-SES children suffer the most in this situation, for the middle-class children who have reading difficulties are often taken elsewhere by their parents for services (for example, to a university clinic or center for a diagnosis) and provided with a private tutor.

A major confusion about the teaching of reading concerns whether reading is essentially the same at different levels or whether it changes as it develops. The findings from this study support the theory that reading changes over time, and that a major transition point comes at about grade 4. Many in the field of reading, however, believe that reading is a single-stage process—that it is essentially the same for the beginner in grade 1 and for the more advanced reader in grade 4 and beyond. This single-stage view of reading places equal focus on all components from the start—cognition, language, and reading skills. Our position is that a single-stage view of reading makes it difficult to focus instruction on the essential elements of each level and to assess whether students are advancing as expected.

Focus on "high-level" skills (comprehension, word meanings, and inference) in the primary grades might limit time that should be devoted to word recognition and decoding—the main tasks in beginning reading. Although such practices might work well with middle-class children whose parents and tutors can help them with what the school might fail to teach, they are particularly detrimental to low-income children, who do not get as much assistance at home and who rely more on the school for their learning.

With a single-stage view of reading, teachers in the intermediate and upper elementary grades may not be aware that they need to make special provision for vocabulary learning, particularly for the low-income children. Although such children know and do not need practice with the concrete, familiar words found in the primary grade texts, they do need help in learning the more unfamiliar, literary, abstract, and specialized vocabularies that are used in texts beginning around grade 4. Again, middle-class, mainstream children will not lose as much as at-risk children if such instruction is missing, because they acquire more of these words from being read to and from reading more outside of school.

It appears, then, that even though we have the knowledge to help prevent the deceleration of literacy achievement among low-income children, we are still far from providing what is needed. The time to examine the conditions that keep many schools from providing the programs that all children need—and especially those at risk—is now.

EPILOGUE

Persistent Questions

Certain questions about the literacy development of low-income children persist over time; although interest in them waxes and wanes, they remain issues of concern. In this final chapter, we formulate responses to these questions based on our own findings.

1. *Is the reading problem that low-income children face essentially one of language, cognition, or reading skill development?*

The youngest children in our study had the linguistic, cognitive, and reading skill abilities necessary for success in the primary grades. They were on a par with a normative population of second and third graders in reading. Furthermore, they received the highest possible scores on many of our language tests, indicating good control of several aspects of English syntax. In writing, although their form was poor, the content of their essays was, in general, quite good.

The first and largest decelerations in the middle grades occurred with word meaning, word recognition, and spelling tasks, rather than in thinking or aspects of language. The problems of these children were quite specific to the reading and writing skills that are generally learned in school.

2. *Can the fourth-grade slump be prevented?*

Our findings indicate several ways in which the fourth-grade slump may be prevented or ameliorated. First, we must address the problem of these children's vocabularies, which do not seem to grow adequately after the third grade. Attention must be paid to the fact that low-income children do not seem to acquire many of the more sophisticated, abstract, specialized, and literary words needed for academic success in the intermediate and later elementary grades. They must be provided with opportunities to read many books—reading textbooks and subject-matter textbooks as well as trade books—books on many topics and books that stretch their abilities. When materials are challenging (somewhat above the students' present achievement), teachers must provide appropriate instruction. When challenging materials are accompanied by such instruction, children in elementary school are most likely to grow in vocabulary as well as in word recognition and reading comprehension.

Attention must also be paid to developing accuracy and fluency of word recognition. Instructional attention to these basic reading skills should begin in the early grades because they not only foster the development of meaningful reading but also facilitate earlier independent reading of more difficult stories and informational books—sources of vocabulary development. Attention to these skills should be maintained during the middle grades in order to ensure that the achievements of the first three grades constitute a foundation for continued growth in decoding, comprehension, and automaticity.

3. *When should the reading difficulties of low-income children be addressed?*

Our findings indicate that they should be addressed as soon as they occur. Waiting for reading difficulties to correct themselves may lead to even greater problems. Our results suggest that children who have problems early develop more serious problems later; thus, an unattended lag of six months in grade 4 may mean a lag of two or more years in grades 6 or 7 and greater lags in high school. Early assessment and help are crucial to prevent snowballing of weaknesses.

4. *Is the home or the school more important in the literacy development of low-income children?*

Both are important; and, in the early grades, home and school each seem to be able to compensate for weaknesses in the other. Low-income children seem to do better in the early grades when *both* the home and the school provide optimal conditions for literacy development. Those who experience optimal environments in only the home or the school still seem to do well. In those cases where both the home and the school environments are weak, however, the children experience serious difficulty with literacy development.

In the middle and upper elementary grades, fewer of the low-income families in our study had the educational and literacy attainment necessary to help their children with school work. Thus, in the fourth grade and beyond, when the literacy and language development of the low-income children began to decelerate and their homes could not provide the help they needed, the role of the school became more important.

5. Does the reading of low-income children develop differently from that of children from middle-income homes?

Our findings indicate that low-income and middle-income children are quite similar in their reading development. In our study, the low-income children in grades 2 and 3 achieved in reading on a level similar to that of the larger population. Even in grade 6, more than half of the low-income children were somewhat above grade level in reading. The below-average readers were generally the ones who were below grade level in grade 4 and even more severely behind in grades 6 and 7. However, when these same students were in classes that provided structured, direct, and challenging learning activities as well as varied materials, they made more than the expected year's gain in one year.

Middle-class children, even those from highly literate and stimulating homes, may also lag behind the normal population in reading. As with low-income children, difficulties with the mechanical aspects of reading (decoding, word recognition, or fluency), as well as with vocabulary meanings, ultimately affect the more cognitive components of their reading (reading comprehension).

The key, then, to the continued growth of literacy in low-income children, as in all children, is to assess their progress regularly and address areas of weakness as soon as they are identified. The needs of low-income children are not essentially different from those of children from middle-class homes. Indeed, our findings suggest that low-income children benefit most from programs that work best for most children—a strong reading program that provides for learning of skills as well as wide reading in the primary grades, and a combination of structure, challenging and direct teaching, and practice in the reading of many books on a wide variety of topics in the middle grades.

We conclude with a sense of optimism, for we found many strengths in the low-income children we studied. Especially in the primary grades, their home and school influences were adequate for them to achieve reading scores comparable to a normative population. They were taught well, and they achieved well.

The lags they experienced in the intermediate and upper elementary grades, beginning at grade 4, make sense in light of the increased educational demands in these grades and the decreased literacy stimulation they received at home and in school. However, when classrooms did provide the instruction and the literate environments needed for making the transition to the more mature reading of the intermediate and upper elementary grades, these children learned well. Such classrooms supplied the children with sufficient and appropriate textbooks, reference works, library books, and writing materials. These classroom environments and instructional programs were essentially the same as those that have been found effective for mainstream children in grades 4 and beyond. Thus, the basic knowledge and techniques for developing the literacy of low-income children are already known; what needs to be done is to make them more widely available. It is an investment for our country's future that we cannot afford to ignore.

Appendixes · References · Index

APPENDIX A

Samples of Narrative Writing Representing Average Holistic Ratings and Production: Students' Handwriting

SHes going To Open it
SHes holding iT up
SHes at a STore and SHes going To byit
SHes going home and eating it

ALN1

This old lady has bot some tomatoes.
And the store man thinks she stool them.
He has called the police. And the old lady
is very fritand. And soon the police cones.
And ask here a lot of things like were did she
get the tomatoes, what is her name, where
do she liv,. And she answerd all of then
exsept for two and thay ware were she liv
and what her name was.

KBN1

This is a woman that is going to buy some
tomatoes. She is looking back to see if any body is
coming. So she can grab alot becaus they are
on sale, and the are ripe and big. If she dont get
any now. she will never get them agan.

the end

RMN1

The woman has some tomatoes.
and she is looking at somone
to throe them at.
there are three tomatoes coverd with
a plastic sheet. the old woman has glasses
and a string of pearls. and a new dress.
with stars on them.

PJN2

This is am old lady looking for Some
big red Juicy tomatoe's. She is going to
bye Some tomatoes. She when She get's home
She might make Salad to eat for lunth, She
also might be Picking up some tomtoe's for
here Son's wife or a frend. After may be
a week after She will go back and get
Some more juicy tomatoes to eat or maybe
lettuce this time. She might not even
get vegativbles any more She might get
Some nice lene meat. and have a cook out
and have meat, coke, hamburgers, hotdogs and
fruit Punch.

AJN2

This is a picture of a old lady who is
about to buy some tamatoes but she yelling
and screaming about how expansive they are
so she standing there wondering if she should
buy or not so she decided to buy the
tamatoes olny for half price but if
she did that she would not be aloned
in that paticular store anymore. So she
went along with the idea of not
being able to go in the store anymore.

CTN2

APPENDIX B

Samples of Expository Writing Representing Average Holistic Ratings and Production: Students' Handwriting

I admire my Farther
cose wen um Faling bad
makes me Fale Better
and he's a good
persing he buys me
Stuf like a bike

JFE1

I looke up to my mother and my farther
because are the ones that beat all those. T.V. Stars
the storr book people. and the sports people.
And you can trust them with out a dout
and if thay gave me some thing thay wo'nt
be ersepthig any thing back from me. I realle
don't know what that word means.
but what they do for me I really admire
them for

BKE1

I look up to my friend [redacted] she is very smart and she is friendly, I like her family there are nice espiacialy her grandmother she nice to me and my family. She always has alot of ideas that make sences that why I look up to her.

DWE1

The Boston redSox are My favret
bass ball players
the best one I like is jim rise
I like how he hit's tose home run's
and I like caw it scemsky and he hit's
home run's to
but the best one is Me

MHE2

I edmire my carisin becase when ever i'm intruoble she sticks up for me.
My causins name is [redacted]
She realys gets me out of trouble most of the time. and when ever I pick kids she tells me not to pick on then why don't you pick on some one your one sire. thats how come I admire cosin. Thats how come I stick a round with her. one tine when we were at. [redacted] park I kept throwing pennies at people she said you beter stop it or were going home. and I would stop.

GFE2

The puson that I admire is a good friend of mine she has long black hair and is very pretty. She is very nice we do alot of things. together. We always have fun were ever we go I like when we go to the movies on saturday night with a couple of other people. But the really only other reason why I like █████ is because we never fight like me and my other friends.

TCE2

References

Adams, M. J. 1989. *Beginning to read: Thinking and learning about print.*. Cambridge, Mass.: MIT Press.

Anderson, R. C., and P. Freebody. 1981. Vocabulary knowledge. In *Comprehension and teaching: Research reviews,* ed. J. T. Guthrie. Newark, Del.: International Reading Association.

Anderson, R. C., E. H. Hiebert, J. A. Scott, and I. A. G. Wilkinson. 1985. *Becoming a nation of readers: The report of the Commission on Reading.* Champaign, Ill.: The Center for the Study of Reading and The National Academy of Education.

Applebee, A. N., J. A. Langer, and I. V. S. Mullis. 1987. *Learning to be literate in America: Reading, writing, and reasoning.* Princeton, N.J.: National Assessment of Educational Progress, Educational Testing Service.

——— 1988. *Who reads best? Factors related to reading achievement in grades 3, 7, and 11.* Princeton, N.J.: National Assessment of Educational Progress, Educational Testing Service.

——— 1989. *Crossroads in American education.* Princeton, N.J.: National Assessment of Educational Progress, Educational Testing Service.

Au, K. H-P. 1980. Participation structures in a reading lesson with Hawaiian children. *Anthropology and Education Quarterly* 11:91–115.

Au, K. H-P., and C. Jordan. 1981. Teaching reading to Hawaiian children: Finding a culturally appropriate solution. In *Culture and the bilingual classroom,* ed. H. Trueba, G. P. Guthrie, and K. H-P. Au. Rowley, Mass.: Newbury House Publishers.

Auerbach, I. T. 1971. Analysis of standardized reading comprehension tests. Ed.D. diss., Harvard University Graduate School of Education.

Baldwin, L. 1986. A description and evaluation of a community based reading program for low income children. Ed.D. diss., Harvard University Graduate School of Education.

Baratz, J. C., and R. Shuy. 1969. *Teaching black children to read.* Washington, D.C.: Center for Applied Linguistics.

Bell, R., and E. Schaefer. 1957. The parental attitude research instrument.

Washington, D.C.: National Institute of Mental Health, Department of Health, Education, and Welfare.

Bereiter, C., and S. Engelmann. 1966. *Teaching disadvantaged children in the preschool.* Englewood Cliffs, N.J.: Prentice-Hall.

Bereiter, C., and M. Scardamalia. 1982. From conversation to composition: The role of instruction in a developmental process. In *Advances in instructional psychology,* vol. 2, ed. R. Glaser. Hillsdale, N.J.: Lawrence Erlbaum Associates.

Bernstein, B. 1959. A public voice: Some sociological implications of a linguistic form. *British Journal of Sociology* 10:311–326.

——— 1960. Language and social class. *British Journal of Sociology* 11:271–276.

——— 1971. *Class, codes, and control.* Vol. 1, *Theoretical studies towards a sociology of language.* London: Routledge & Kegan Paul.

Berrueta-Clement, J. R., I. J. Schweinhart, W. S. Barnett, A. S. Epstein, and D. P. Weikart. 1984. *Changed lives: The effects of the Perry Preschool Program on youths through age 19.* Ypsilanti, Mich.: High/Scope Press.

Berry, M. 1977. New emphases in federal policy on education. *Phi Delta Kappan* 59:122–126.

Berthoff, A. E. 1984. The most important development in the last five years for high school teachers of composition. *English Journal* 73:20.

Blank, M., S. A. Rose, and L. J. Berlin. 1978. *The language of learning: The preschool years.* New York: Grune & Stratton.

Bledsoe, J. C. 1959. An investigation of six correlates of student withdrawal from high school. *Journal of Educational Research* 53:3–6.

Bloom, B. S. 1976. *Human characteristics and school learning.* New York: McGraw-Hill.

Boggs, S. T. 1972. The meaning of questions and narratives to Hawaiian children. In *Functions of language in the classroom,* ed. C. Cazden, V. John, and D. Hymes. New York: Teachers College Press.

Buswell, G. T. 1922. *Fundamental reading habits: A study of their development.* Supplementary Educational Monographs no. 21. Chicago: University of Chicago Department of Education.

Caldwell, B. M. 1987. Staying ahead: The challenge of the third-grade slump. *Principal* 66(5):10–14.

Calkins, L. M. 1986. *The art of teaching writing.* Portsmouth, N.H.: Heinemann.

Carroll, J. B. 1971. Development of native language skills beyond the early years. In *The learning of language,* ed. C. Read. New York: Appleton Century Croft.

——— 1977. Developmental parameters of reading comprehension. In *Cognition, curriculum, and comprehension,* ed. J. T. Guthrie. Newark, Del.: International Reading Association.

Caswell, H. L. 1933. Non-promotion in the elementary school. *Elementary School Journal* 33:644–647.

Cazden, C. 1987. The myth of autonomous text. Paper presented at the Third International Conference on Thinking, Hawaii, January 1987.

Chall, J. S. 1967. *Learning to read: The great debate*. New York: McGraw-Hill.

——— 1969. Research in linguistics and reading instruction: Implications for further research and practice. In *Reading and realism,* vol. 13, part 1, Proceedings of the thirteenth annual convention, ed. J. A. Figurel. Newark, Del.: International Reading Association.

——— 1979. The great debate: Ten years later, with a modest proposal for reading stages. In *Theory and practice of early reading,* ed. L. Resnick and P. Weaver. Hillsdale, N.J.: Lawrence Erlbaum Associates.

——— 1983a. *Learning to read: The great debate,* updated edition. New York: McGraw-Hill.

——— 1983b. *Stages of reading development*. New York: McGraw-Hill.

——— 1986. School and teacher factors and the NAEP reading assessments. Paper commissioned by the Study Group on the National Assessment of Student Achievement and cited in Appendix B to their final report, *The nation's report card,* August 1986. ERIC Document Reproduction Service no. ED 279 667.

——— 1987. The importance of instruction in reading methods for all teachers. In *Intimacy with language: A forgotten basic in teacher education*. Baltimore: The Orton Dyslexia Society.

——— 1989a. Could the decline be real? Recent trends in reading instruction and support in the U.S. In *Report of the NAEP Technical Review Panel on the 1986 reading anomaly, the accuracy of NAEP trends, and issues raised by state-level NAEP comparisons*. Washington, D.C.: National Center for Education Statistics and U.S. Department of Education.

——— 1989b. *Learning to read: The great debate* 20 years later: A response to "Debunking the great phonics myth." *Phi Delta Kappan* 70:521–538.

Chall, J. S., S. S. Conard, and S. Harris. 1977. *An analysis of textbooks in relation to declining S.A.T. scores*. New York: College Entrance Examination Board.

Chall, J. S., S. S. Conard, and S. Harris-Sharples. 1983. *Textbooks and challenge: An inquiry into textbook difficulty, reading achievement, and knowledge acquisition*. A final report to the Spencer Foundation. Cambridge, Mass.: Harvard University Graduate School of Education.

Chall, J. S., and M. E. Curtis. 1987. What clinical diagnosis tells us about children's reading. *The Reading Teacher* 40:784–788.

Chall, J. S., and S. Feldmann. 1966. First grade reading: An analysis of the interactions of professed methods, teacher implementation and child background. *The Reading Teacher* 19:569–575.

Chall, J. S., and R. W. Peterson. 1986. The influence of neuroscience upon educational practice. In *The brain, cognition, and education,* ed. S. L. Friedman, K. A. Klivington, and R. W. Peterson. Orlando, Fla.: Academic Press.

Chall, J. S., C. Snow, W. S. Barnes, J. Chandler, I. F. Goodman, L. Hemphill, and V. Jacobs. 1982. *Families and literacy: The contribution of out-of-school experiences to children's acquisition of literacy.* Final report to the National Institute of Education, December 22, 1982. ERIC Document Reproduction Service no. ED 234 345.

Chall, J. S., and S. A. Stahl. 1985. Reading comprehension research in the last decade: Implications for educational publishing. *Book Research Quarterly* 1:95–102.

Chandler, J., and Hemphill, L. 1983. Models of classrooms as effective literacy environments for low-income children. Unpublished ms., Harvard Graduate School of Education.

Chomsky, C. 1972. Stages in language development and reading exposure. *Harvard Educational Review* 42:1–33.

——— 1978. When you still can't read in the third grade: After decoding, what? In *What research has to say about reading instruction,* ed. S. J. Samuels. Newark, Del.: International Reading Association.

Cohen, S. 1969. *Teach them all to read.* New York: Random House.

Coleman, J. S., E. Campbell, C. Hobson, J. McPartland, A. Mood, F. Weinfeld, and R. York. 1966. *Equality of educational opportunity.* Washington, D.C.: U.S. Government Printing Office.

Conard, S. S. 1981. The difficulty of textbooks for the elementary grades: A survey of educators' and publishers' preferences. Ed.D. diss., Harvard University Graduate School of Education.

Cooper, C. R., and L. Odell. 1977. *Evaluating writing: Describing, measuring, judging.* Urbana, Ill.: National Council of Teachers of English.

Currier, L. B. 1923. Phonics and no phonics. *Elementary School Journal* 23:448–452.

Curtis, M. E. 1986. The National Assessment of Reading: Past and future directions. Paper commissioned by the Study Group on the National Assessment of Student Achievement and cited in Appendix B to their final report, *The nation's report card,* August, 1986. ERIC Document Reproduction Service no. Ed 279 667.

Dale, E., and J. S. Chall. 1948. *A formula for predicting readability.* Columbus, Ohio: Ohio State University Bureau of Educational Research. (Reprinted from *Educational Research Bulletin* 27:11–20, 37–54.)

Dale, E., and J. O'Rourke. 1971. *Techniques of teaching vocabulary.* Chicago: Field Educational Publications.

——— 1981. *The living word vocabulary.* Chicago: World Book-Childcraft International.

Daniels, J. C., and H. Diack. 1956. *Progress in reading.* Nottingham, England: Institute of Education, University of Nottingham.

——— 1960. *Progress in reading in the infant school.* Nottingham, England: Institute of Education, University of Nottingham.

Dave, R. H. 1963. The identification and measurement of environmental process variables that are related to educational achievement. Ph.D. diss., University of Chicago.

Davis, F. B. 1968. Research in comprehension in reading. *Reading Research Quarterly* 3:499–545.

——— 1972. Psychometric research on comprehension in reading. In *Final report: The literature of research in reading with emphasis on models,* ed. F. B. Davis. New Brunswick, N.J.: Graduate School of Education, Rutgers University.

Delpit, L. D. 1988. When the talking stops: Paradoxes of power in educating other people's children. Paper presented at the Ninth Annual Ethnography in Education Research Forum, University of Pennsylvania, February 1988.

Deutsch, C. P. 1964. Auditory discrimination and learning: Social factors. *Merrill-Palmer Quarterly* 10:277–296.

Diederich, P. B., ed. 1974. *Measuring growth in English.* Urbana, Ill.: National Council of Teachers of English.

Durkin, D. 1982. *A study of poor black children who are successful readers.* Reading Education Report no. 33. Champaign, Ill.: Center for the Study of Reading, University of Illinois at Urbana-Champaign.

Edmonds, R. 1979. Effective schools for the urban poor. *Educational Leadership* 37:15–24.

Ehri, L. C. 1987. Learning to read and spell words. *Journal of Reading Behavior* 19:5–30.

Empey, L. 1956. Social class and occupational aspiration: A comparison of absolute and relative measurements. *American Sociological Review* 21:703–709.

Fagan, W. T., C. R. Cooper, and J. Jensen. 1975. Measures: writing. In *Measures for research and evaluation in the English language arts,* ed. W. T. Fagan, C. R. Cooper, and J. Jensen. Urbana, Ill.: National Council of Teachers of English.

Flower, L. S., and J. R. Hayes. 1980. The dynamics of composing: Making plans and juggling constraints. In *Cognitive processes in writing,* ed. L. W. Gregg and E. R. Steinberg. Hillsdale, N.J.: Lawrence Erlbaum Associates.

Fowles, M. E. 1978. *Basic skills assessment: Manual for scoring the writing sample.* Princeton, N.J.: Educational Testing Service.

Freebody, P., and B. Byrne. 1988. Word-reading strategies in elementary school children: Relations to comprehension, reading time, and phonemic awareness. *Reading Research Quarterly* 23:441–453.

Goodman, I. F., and L. Hemphill. 1982. Home factors associated with superior reading achievement among low income children. Paper presented at 20th Congress of Applied Psychology, Edinburgh, July 1982.

Graves, D. 1983. *Writing: Teachers and children at work.* Portsmouth, N.H.: Heinemann.

Graves, M. F. 1987. The roles of instruction in fostering vocabulary development. In *The nature of vocabulary acquisition,* ed. M. G. McKeown and M. E. Curtis. Hillsdale, N.J.: Lawrence Erlbaum Associates.

Gray Oral Reading Test. 1963. New York: Bobbs-Merrill.

Haller, E. P., D. A. Child, and H. J. Walberg. 1988. Can comprehension be taught? A quantitative synthesis of "metacognitive" studies. *Educational Researcher* 17(9):5–8.

Hammill, D., and S. Larsen. 1978. *Test of written language.* Austin, Tex.: Pro-Ed.

Harris, A. J. 1961. *How to increase reading ability,* 4th ed. New York: Longman.

Harris-Sharples, S. H. 1983. A study of the "match" between student reading ability and textbook difficulty during classroom instruction. Ed.D. diss., Harvard University Graduate School of Education.

Heath, S. B. 1983. *Ways with words.* New York: Cambridge University Press.

Hemphill, L., and I. F. Goodman. 1982. Classroom factors associated with superior reading achievement among low income children. Paper presented at 20th Congress of Applied Psychology, Edinburgh, July 1982.

Hill, E. H., and M. C. Giammatteo. 1963. Socio-economic status and its relationship to school achievement in the elementary school. *Elementary English* 40:265–270.

Hillocks, G. 1986. *Research on written composition: New directions for teaching.* Urbana, Ill.: ERIC Clearinghouse on Reading and Communication Skills.

Holmes, J. A. 1976. Basic assumptions underlying the substrata-factor theory. In *Theoretical models and processes of reading,* ed. H. Singer and R. B. Ruddell. Newark, Del.: International Reading Association.

Hornik, R. 1978. Television access and the slowing of cognitive growth. *American Educational Research Journal* 15(1):1–15.

——— 1981. Out-of-school television and schooling: Hypotheses and methods. *Review of Educational Research* 51:193–214.

Hunt, K. 1965. *Grammatical structures written at three grade levels.* National Council of Teachers of English Research Report no. 3. Urbana, Ill.: National Council of Teachers of English.

Irwin, O. C. 1948. Infant speech: The effect of family occupational status and of age on use of sound types. *Journal of Speech and Hearing Disorders* 13:224–226.

Jacobs, V. A. 1986. The use of connectives in low-income, elementary children's writing and its relation to their reading, writing, and language skill development. Ed.D. diss., Harvard University Graduate School of Education.

Jencks, C., et al. 1972. *Inequality: A reassessment of the effect of family and schooling in America.* New York: Basic Books.

Johnson, D. D., and P. D. Pearson. 1984. *Teaching reading vocabulary,* 2nd ed. New York: Holt, Rinehart and Winston.

Juel, C. 1988. Learning to read and write: A longitudinal study of fifty-four children from first through fourth grades. *Journal of Educational Psychology* 80:437–447.

Karger, G. W. 1973. The performance of lower class black and lower class white children on the Wepman Auditory Discrimination Test: The effects of dialect and training, and the relationship to reading achievement. Ed.D. diss., Harvard University Graduate School of Education.

LaBerge, D., and S. J. Samuels. 1976. Toward a theory of automatic information processing in reading. In *Theoretical models and processes of reading,* ed. H. Singer and R. B. Ruddell. Newark, Del.: International Reading Association.

Labov, W. 1972. *Language in the inner city.* Philadelphia: University of Pennsylvania Press.

Loban, W. 1963. *The language of elementary school children.* National Council of Teachers of English Research Report no. 1. Urbana, Ill.: National Council of Teachers of English.

——— 1976. *Language development: Kindergarten through grade twelve.* National Council of Teachers of English Research Report no. 18. Urbana, Ill.: National Council of Teachers of English.

Lovell, K., and M. E. Woolsey. 1964. Reading disability, nonverbal reasoning, and social class. *British Journal of Educational Research* 6:226–227.

MacDonald, D. P. 1963. An investigation of the attitudes of parents of unsuccessful and successful readers. *Journal of Educational Research* 56:437–438.

Malmquist, E. 1960. Factors related to reading disabilities in the first grade. In *Stockholm Studies in Educational Psychology.* Stockholm: Almquist and Wiksell.

Marston, E. 1982. An investigation of variables relating to the voluntary reading habits of eighth graders. Ed.D. diss., Harvard University Graduate School of Education.

Meyer, L. A. 1989. *Interim report of trends from a longitudinal study of the development of reading comprehension ability.* Champaign, Ill.: Center for the Study of Reading, University of Illinois at Urbana-Champaign.

Montessori, M. 1964. *The Montessori method.* New York: Schocken Books.

Myklebust, H. R. 1965. *Development and disorders of written language.* Vol. 1, *Picture story language test.* New York: Grune & Stratton.

Nagy, W. B. 1989. *Teaching vocabulary to improve reading comprehension.* Newark, Del.: International Reading Association, National Council of Teachers of English, and ERIC Clearinghouse.

National Assessment of Educational Progress (NAEP). 1971. *1969–1970 Writing: Group results for sex, region, and size of community.* Washington, D.C.: U.S. Government Printing Office.

——— 1972. *Reading rate and comprehension.* Report 02-R-09. Washington, D.C.: U.S. Government Printing Office.

——— 1981. *Three national assessments: Changes in performance, 1970–80.* Denver, Colo.: Education Commission of the States.

——— 1985. *The reading report card: Progress toward excellence in our schools.* Princeton, N.J.: Educational Testing Service.

Nice, M. M. 1915. The development of a child's vocabulary in relation to environment. *Pedagogical Seminary* 22:34–64.

O'Donnell, R. C., W. J. Griffin, and R. C. Norris. 1967. *Syntax of kindergarten and elementary school children: A transformational analysis.* National Council of Teachers of English Research Report no. 8. Urbana, Ill.: National Council of Teachers of English.

Orton, S. T. 1937 (reprinted 1964). *Reading, writing, and speech problems in children.* New York: W. W. Norton.

Parker, R. P., Jr. 1979. From Sputnik to Dartmouth: Trends in the teaching of composition. *English Journal* 65:42–46.

Perfetti, C. A. 1985. *Reading ability.* New York: Oxford University Press.

Rist, R. C. 1970. Student social class and teacher expectations: The self-fulfilling prophecy in ghetto education. *Harvard Educational Review* 40:411–451.

Roswell, F. G., and J. S. Chall. In press. *Diagnostic Assessment of Reading and Teaching Strategies.* Chicago: Riverside Publishing Company.

Shaughnessy, M. P. 1977. *Errors and expectations: A guide for the teacher of basic writing.* New York: Oxford University Press.

Simons, H. 1979. Black dialect, reading interference, and classroom interaction. In *Theory and practice of early reading,* vol. 3, ed. L. Resnick and P. Weaver. Hillsdale, N.J.: Lawrence Erlbaum Associates.

Singer, H. 1962. Substrata-factor theory of reading: Theoretical design for the teaching of reading. In *Challenge and experiment in reading: International Reading Association proceedings,* ed. J. A. Figurel. Newark, Del.: International Reading Association.

Snow, C. E., W. S. Barnes, J. Chandler, I. F. Goodman, and L. Hemphill. Forthcoming. *Unfulfilled expectations: Home and school influences on literacy.*

Spache, G. 1974. The revised Spache readability formula. In G. Spache, *Good reading for poor readers.* Champaign, Ill.: Garrard Publishing Company.

Stahl, S. A., and P. D. Miller. 1989. Whole language and language experience approaches for beginning reading: A quantitative research synthesis. *Review of Educational Research* 59:87–116.

Stallings, J. 1975. *Implementation and child effects of teaching practices in Follow-Through classrooms.* Monograph of the Society for Research in Child Development. Serial no. 163, vol. 40, no. 7–8.

Stanovich, K. E. 1982. Word recognition skill and reading ability. In *Competent reader, disabled reader: Research and application,* ed. M. Singer. Hillsdale, N.J.: Lawrence Erlbaum Associates.

——— 1986. Matthew effects in reading: Some consequences of individual differences in the acquisition of literacy. *Reading Research Quarterly* 21:360–407.

Stotsky, S. L. 1984. Imagination, writing, and the integration of knowledge in the middle grades. *Journal of Teaching Writing* 3:157–190.

Terman, L. M., and M. Lima. 1926. *Children's reading.* New York: Appleton-Century.

Thorndike, E. L. 1917. Reading as reasoning: A study of mistakes in paragraph reading. *Journal of Educational Research* 8:323–332.

Thorndike, R. L. 1973. *Reading comprehension education in fifteen countries.* International Studies in Evaluation III. Stockholm, Sweden: Almquist and Wiksell.

——— 1973–74. Reading as reasoning. *Reading Research Quarterly* 9:135–147.

Vygotsky, L. S. 1962. *Thought and language,* ed. and trans. E. Hanfmann and G. Vakar. Cambridge, Mass.: MIT Press.

Weber, G. 1971. *Inner-city children can be taught to read.* Washington, D.C.: Council for Basic Education.

Wechsler, D. 1971. *Wechsler Intelligence Scale for Children—Revised* (WISC-R). New York: The Psychological Corporation.

Weiner, M., and S. Feldmann. 1963. Validation studies of a reading prognosis test for children of lower and middle socioeconomic status. *Educational and Psychological Measurement* 23:807–814.

Wide Range Achievement Test (WRAT). 1978. Wilmington, Del.: Jastak Associates.

Index